Esse

Essential Zen

Edited by
Kazuaki Tanahashi
and
Tensho David Schneider

Brushwork by
Kazuaki Tanahashi

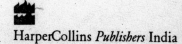

HarperCollins *Publishers* India

HarperCollins *Publishers* India Pvt Ltd
7/16 Ansari Road, Daryaganj, New Delhi 110 002

First Published 1995 by
HarperCollins *Publishers* Inc.

First published in India 1996 by HarperCollins *Publishers* India

© Kazuaki Tanahashi & David Schneider 1994

© Illustrations by Kazuaki Tanahashi 1994

ISBN 0-06-251047-9

By arrangement with
HarperCollins, San Francisco

All texts are reproduced with permission.
Acknowledgements begin in the Notes, page 145.

Printed in India by
Gopsons Papers Ltd
A-28, Sector IX
Noida 201 301

Contents

On Positive Emptiness

STORIES REMAIN in our consciousness, often unnoticed, as points of reference for understanding elements of life. However weird or enigmatic they are, or perhaps because of those very qualities, Zen stories have touched the hearts of people for over a thousand years.

One of the most frequently quoted stories in the West seems to be one about a person who went to see a Zen master with a load of questions and arguments. The master kept on pouring tea into a cup for the guest until it started overflowing. To the panicked guest, the master said, "If your mind is already filled like this, how can there be room for you to learn?" This seemingly unrealistic story was introduced in Paul Reps's *Zen Flesh Zen Bones*. Presenting a certain truth about learning, this story illustrates a paradox—the power of what might be called "positive emptiness."

We all tend to possess, accumulate, store, and consume, trying to have as much influence and control as possible in our daily lives. This produces a great deal of anxiety, which in turn creates a longing for freedom from such a mode of clinging. Sooner or later we may come to understand that we are free when we are not preoccupied, that we receive more by letting go, and that we achieve more by being selfless. This is the dynamics of nonpossession, which is an essential part of the creative process in the Zen world.

Another important Zen story, although not so well known, describes Shunryu Suzuki on his deathbed silently drawing a circle in the air after a student asks him where they will meet in the future. This traditional gesture may be interpreted as a message about a meditative experience of transcending here and there, lack and abundance, life and death. The master may have been suggesting that nothing matters other than living at the very moment with full intensity and joy. Many Zen stories and poems point to dealing with the matter of life and death directly, rather than depending on the hope for heaven, the Pure Land, or reincarnation. A Zen circle is regarded as an expression of enlightenment—an experience of completeness—at each moment. The circle is unique for each individual, for each moment, just as it is unique every time it is drawn with a brush.

The incident described in a story occurs in a particular place at a particular time among a small number of people, or in someone's imagination. But once it is developed as a pointer to awakening, it can be pondered by innumerable seekers of the Way for hundreds of years. A poem that was originally scribbled in a mountain hut in China can be recited daily in monasteries all over East Asia. Thus a certain core of Zen literature has entered what might be called the collective consciousness of the tradition. Some of the ancient sayings and writings collected in this book have survived such a process.

We are living in an exciting time in the history of Zen, as it is becoming an indispensable part of Western culture. The Zen attempt to break through such conceptual barriers as self and other, sentient and nonsentient beings, is merging with the egalitarian and democratic views of the West. Works by Gary Snyder, Robert Aitken, Thich Nhat Hanh, and Joan Halifax provide inspiration from Zen Buddhist thought for those who are engaged in peace and environmental work. The source of this influence is not limited to Zen but comes from Buddhism in general as well as from an awareness of the interconnectedness of all being. The message of pioneers in the understanding of deep ecology reminds us that we cannot fully experience each moment with positive emptiness unless we participate in changing the social situations that are harming living beings and the environment.

If the present moment is when truth is actually experienced, then Western Zen, however young and immature, ought to be treated on a par with traditional Zen in China, Korea, and Japan. The process of editing this book has confirmed our sense that the Western contribution to Zen is enormous and admirable. Many materials from American Zen sources are included here. Because of our location in the United States, we haven't been able to collect as much from non-Asian places as we might have liked.

This is a personal collection of Zen sayings and writings; many of the stories and poems have had profound meaning for the editors. We hope that you, in reading it, will feel that you are in a vast community of seekers of the Way, with diverse backgrounds, coming from different moments in history, able to make you smile, laugh, or reflect.

Kazuaki Tanahashi

Graffiti on Perfectly Good Paper

THE BOOK you are holding is titled *Essential Zen*—and this title has caused a lot of trouble to its editors. Zen prides itself on being a teaching "outside words and letters"; thus any book of mere writing—no matter how elevated or enlightened—could not rightly be called essential. The essential Zen, in book form, would more likely consist of blank pages; a reader fills them in. Or not.

For about twelve centuries, Zen teachers have warned their students away from literary endeavor. Book learning of any kind has been regarded suspiciously by serious practitioners as a very dim second best to direct experience. And yet an enormous and illuminating Zen literature has grown up. How has this happened?

Sayings and doings of the ancient Chinese masters were originally recorded, usually by a faithful student. These records were discussed, chanted sometimes, codified, and given out as objects of meditation—the renowned *koans,* or spiritual puzzles. When Zen reached Japan and other countries, the same thing happened. It appears that Zen teachers of every age (including the present one) found delight not only in reading what other masters said and did, but in commenting about them, and in collecting their comments into books. These new books have then been fair game for further commentary by other teachers, and so on.

The Zen lineages have thus enshrined an ambivalence about books like this one. Officially, they are discouraged; actually, they multiply. Welcome to Zen tradition.

But *essential* Zen? As some readers are no doubt aware, the word *Zen* is Japanese for the Chinese word *ch'an,* which in turn is a transliteration of the Sanskrit word *dhyana,* all of them meaning "meditation." Among the various practitioners of Buddhism, Zen people are the meditators. Clearly, any book of essential Zen must include teachings on meditation.

In addition, the person who teaches you how to meditate and who guides you through the numerous pitfalls is usually regarded as valuable. Student-teacher relationships are at the heart of true Zen practice. By extension, Zen students have generally thought it necessary to be part of a lineage, one stretching back to the Buddha himself. Though this view is coming under review and criticism in the most recent rounds of American teaching, it has profoundly informed most of Zen history.

The teacher, the techniques, and then the physical work of supporting the whole situation properly—these are the essential ingredients for carrying out Zen practice. But why would a person want to bother? Zen's reputation for being fierce, uncompromising, demanding, and painful at times is justly deserved. What pushes people to submit to such treatment?

For some, it is the face of death looming steadily closer; others quest for an enlightenment experience; still others meditate to resolve fundamental questions that have somehow pierced them. The Buddha himself was prodded from the comforts of princely life by these very questions, and they've been much discussed in Zen circles ever since. Inasmuch as they've provided incentives to begin meditation, and have been the goads to continue through periods of dullness or fatigue, these issues could also rightly be called essential to Zen.

From its earliest formative days in China, Zen took root then flourished as a monastic system. Though there were highly regarded masters living and teaching outside the institutions, Zen's most characteristic geniuses moved freely among the temples and monasteries, and followed a highly prescribed lifestyle. The strength and tradition of monastic life provided the loom on which the spare, elegant, witty, deadly serious, and humorous fabric of Zen could be woven. Though it would be wrong to say monastic life was essential to all Zen, it *has* been essential to a great deal of the best of it so far.

The point of these remarks is to explain, as far as possible, the "chapter" divisions into which we have placed our selections. When we began to cull through the mountainous Zen texts, themes seemed to arise, and we followed these more or less naturally. Despite such reasoning, it must be admitted that the chapter divisions are secondary, and that a good deal of overlap occurs. It is possible to accurately place many of the stories under one of several headings. These chapters are also a temporary expedient; they helped us organize our material, and we thought they might help a reader in the same way. Beyond that, though, they are not to be taken as solid categories.

An additional thought on the organization of this book: the great Buddhist translator Edward Conze is reported to have said that Zen was simply Mahayana Buddhism plus Chinese jokes. Conze's quip, no doubt intended as another of his famous barbs, contains truth in both its points. Zen has always sprung from the Mahayana, in which the enlightenment and care of others takes precedence over one's own progress. For all its swashbuckling and bravado, Zen is ultimately concerned with the welfare of all sentient beings.

Humor and mischief have always been there too, bubbling up if things got too gloomy or drear. Zen students through the centuries have after all been only human beings with a meditation habit. None of them has been "other" in the sense of coming to practice with a specially fortified body or mind. Everyone has brought basically the same package of thoroughly human qualities to the path. So in our divisions, we've made room both for ideals of selflessness and for sparkles of humor.

If Zen emphasizes anything at all in terms of a "philosophy," it would be *nowness*—the present moment, the present mind. With this as background, we've chosen to include stories of present-day Zen and to put them throughout the book, beside and on equal footing with classic tales of the great Asian masters. This may strike some readers as prideful, or premature at least; it was our clear conviction, however, that another book comprising purely old Chinese and Japanese zenisms would have been a kind of ancestor worship—safe perhaps, but unnecessary, and out of keeping with a fresh Zen spirit.

The decision to include modern stories led us into a thicket of new problems. While Zen itself is always new, and always dawning in each practitioner, it can be introduced to a culture as an exotic religion only once. By the 1960s this introduction had been accomplished in America, largely through the writings of people like D. T. Suzuki, Alan Watts, Lucien Stryk, Paul Reps, Ruth Fuller Sasaki, and the Beat writers, and through the sincere meditation practice of men and women on both coasts.

But the flashy talk of enlightenment, the allure of spare aesthetics, a mystic power in the arts—these initial highlights of Zen were gradually tempered for American students with the mundane realities of board meetings, zoning regulations, fund-raising, health codes, insurance. . . . As Americans steadily practiced traditional Zen forms, they began to see them from the inside, and to inhabit the forms in distinctly new ways. The usual metaphor is that Buddhist teaching flows like water into whatever cultural container it is poured. The actual process seems much more like acid being added to a solid metal bowl: the bowl is etched into a new shape, and the composition of the fluid is made different too.

Zen's past three decades in the West have not been without difficulty. Unlike China and Japan, the West offers no cultural background for Buddhism and certainly no imperial support. Economics have pressed many of the groups sorely. Assumptions about the nature of student-teacher relationships are different here too, in an avowedly democratic, egalitarian society. Disillusionments about this crucial relationship and about issues of sex, money, power, and the dispensation of the teachings have weighed heavily on many, many Zen groups. The selections we've included come from practitioners who have gone through all of this. Their words and styles of expression reflect these experiences, but they also reflect an inspiration bred from just such problems.

For example, an emphasis on justice and social activism has emerged in Western Zen, developing most fully as "engaged Buddhism." Here, practitioners take on social and political causes—not as an extra burden or special practice, but as an integral part of awareness, a natural extension of interconnectedness. Women, who have always figured profoundly in the transmission of Zen wisdom, are at last finding in Western Zen positions of power and authority equal to their merits. We have attempted in our selections to represent both of these fortunate developments.

Because it would have been presumptuous to assume that we alone could determine what in its long history and vast literature was the essential Zen, we asked for help. We sent a letter to all the Zen groups we could find in the United States, and to some in Europe as well, soliciting stories, poems, and anecdotes that seemed to qualify as essential. We made clear that we were interested in stories old and new, renowned or unknown, and many of these submissions found their way into this book. At the same time, we regard *Essential Zen* as the beginning of a conversation with the Western Zen community. We expect that the book will stimulate response and contributions, and that the composition of the material itself may change over time. For us, this is a delightful prospect.

While we have taken pains to be broad and inclusive in *Essential Zen* (given limits of size and scope), we are quite aware that the selection reflects our particular lineage affiliations, and our personal tastes. There is no way around this; we put in what we liked. It seemed to us that in doing so, we were carrying on a long tradition. The koan collections—*Blue Cliff Record (Hekiganroku), Record of Equanimity (Shoyoroku),* and *Gateless Barrier (Mumonkan)*—must all have been compiled in a similar way. That is, the compilers must have put in the stories they thought best, and most useful, and left out others.

By mentioning the koan collections, we do not mean to invite comparison, or to suggest that our purpose here is the same as that of the early compilers. In fact, we have tried to draw very lightly from those anthologies, great though they are. For one thing, the koans have long been published in English and are widely available. We also felt that by putting in dozens of semi-opaque koans, we would be perpetuating a somewhat partial view of Zen. Still, we were unable to resist—after all, these are the masters at their best—and so we retranslated several stories from each collection.

As a reader will soon see, the entries in this book are presented clean; that is, there isn't any accompanying commentary. Biographical information about the main characters and explanatory notes have been put in a reference section. Several people were instrumental in helping us find and sort through this material, and in preparing the manuscript. We gratefully acknowledge the kind help of Taiji Nedelski, Susan Moon, Michael Wenger, and Karen Klussendorf.

Finally, there are the circles running throughout the book. A brushed circle—the *enso*—is a traditional Zen calligraphic motif. It can mean many things: enlightenment, the present, completion. . . . Just as one Zen philosophical tenet would be nowness, one important Zen aesthetic bias would be space. Sometimes you need a mark to point out space.

Tensho David Schneider

Journey

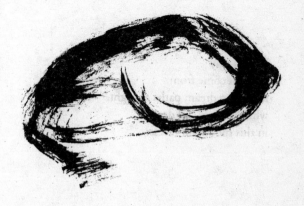

People ask for the road to Cold Mountain,
but no road reaches Cold Mountain.
Summer sky—still ice won't melt.
The sun comes out but gets obscured by mist.
Imitating me, where does that get you?
My mind isn't like yours.
When your mind is like mine
you can enter here.

Hanshan

Which way
did you come from,
following dream paths at night,
while snow is still deep
in this mountain recess?

Ryokan

It was the year 1953 and I had come to Kyoto to find a Zen master, but with no success as yet. While there, I renewed acquaintance with an American professor of philosophy I'd first met while attending Dr. Suzuki's classes at Columbia University. He was a Fulbright exchange scholar and like myself was eager to savor monastery life.

This professor introduced me to the Kyoto Zen academic community, all of whom tried to dissuade us from entering a Zen monastery. "The monasteries are antiquated, the atmosphere cold, the training harsh, and most of the roshis narrow-minded religious zealots," they told us.

But having gotten the name of Zen master Soen Nakagawa from a Japanese acquaintance, we decided, despite their dire warnings, to write and ask if we could stay at his monastery for several weeks. He promptly replied, saying, "Yes, you may come for a week."

On the train to Mishima, where his monastery, Ryutaku-ji, was located, my friend and I composed a series of philosophical questions to "test" the roshi with. "If he answers these questions satisfactorily," we agreed, "let us stay the week; if not, let's leave the next day."

Nakagawa Roshi greeted us warmly upon our arrival, offering us the traditional Zen balm—tea. No sooner had we begun drinking than our questioning erupted. "Stop!" he commanded, throwing up a hand. "After you finish your tea and do zazen for a while, you may ask your questions."

Fair enough. "But how do we do zazen?" we asked. "We've never meditated before."

"Meditate any way you wish, only don't talk."

A monk attendant escorted us to the Buddha Hall and provided sitting cushions, then put a finger to his lips admonishing silence.

For what seemed like an eternity, we thrashed about wildly in a vain effort to cope with the pain and still our restless thoughts. To throw up our hands in despair and stand on our feet would be an admission of defeat, and such a display of weakness might suddenly terminate our stay. So we endured with gritted teeth. At last the monk appeared and mercifully ended our ordeal. "The roshi is waiting for you in his room," he announced with a sardonic smile. We limped to his quarters. The hour was late and we were exhausted. Not having eaten all day, we relished the bowl of rice placed in front of each of us as though it were gourmet food. The roshi, watching us and smiling benignly, said, "Now for the questions."

"No questions, roshi! All we want to do is go to bed."

"Very good idea, because we get up at 3 in the morning."

And that ended my first practical lesson in Zen, a lesson I have never forgotten.

Philip Kapleau

He was offered the whole world,
He declined and turned away.

He did not write poetry,
He lived poetry before it existed.
He did not speak of philosophy,
He cleaned up the dung philosophy left behind.

He had no address:
He lived in a ball of dust playing with the universe.

Jung Kwung

OX

Among other creatures this is what I was.
Abilities depend on the realm; realm also depends on
    abilities.
At birth I forgot completely by which path I came.
I don't know, these years, which school of monk I am.

Ikkyu

Awakened within a dream,
I fall into my own arms.
. . . What kept you so long?

Lou Hartman

Once seventeen monks from Szechwan were traveling, seeking the Way and trying to find a master. Before seeing master Yangshan, they spent the night at his monastery guest house and they began talking about the famous flag story of the Sixth Ancestor. Each of them admitted that they didn't understand it.

Miaoxin, who was the director of the guest house, overheard them talking, and said to herself, "What a pity! These seventeen blind donkeys are wasting their straw sandals. They haven't seen the buddha-dharma, even in their dreams."

A worker heard her comments and told the monks what she'd said. Instead of resenting her comments, the seventeen monks felt humbled. They straightened their robes, burned incense, bowed, and asked Miaoxin for instruction.

The nun said, "Come closer!"

As the monks came forward, she said, "It's not that the wind moves; it's not that the flag moves; it's not that the mind moves."

When they heard this, all seventeen monks understood. They bowed in gratitude and became her students. Then they went back to Szechwan, without even talking to Yangshan.

O

Some old papers were recently excavated
from the ruins of an ancient city
in Eastern Turkestan.
The scholars say that they contain
the thought of Bodhidharma,
and they have been busy turning out commentaries,
both in the horizontal writing of the West

and the vertical lines of the Orient.
Who knows exactly the thought of the blue-eyed monk?
Some imitate his zazen and gaze at the wall
until the sun goes down.
Hey—you are all wrong!

Nyogen Senzaki

Rags and again rags,
wearing rags all my life—
I somehow get food at the side of the road;
my hut is left to overgrown mugwort.
Gazing at the moon all night I chant poems.
Getting lost in flowers I don't come home.
Since leaving my nourishing community,
mistakenly I've become this hobbled old horse.

Ryokan

In winter
the seven stars
walk upon a crystal forest

Soen Nakagawa

We're here to get our present model repainted a little bit. If the car of our life is a deep grey, we want to turn it into lavender or pink. But transformation means that the car may disappear altogether. Maybe instead of a car it will be a turtle. We don't even want to hear of such possibilities. We hope that the teacher will tell us something that will fix our present model. A lot of therapies merely provide techniques for improving the model. They tinker here and there, and we may even feel a lot better. Still, that is not transformation. Transformation arises from a willingness that develops very slowly over time to be what life asks of us.

Most of us (myself included at times) are like children: we want something or somebody to give us what a small child wants from its parents. We want to be given peace, attention, comfort, understanding. If our life doesn't give us this, we think, "A few years of Zen practice will do this for me." No, they won't. That's not what practice is about. Practice is about opening ourselves so that this little "I" that wants and wants and wants and wants and wants—that wants the whole world to be its parents, really—grows up.

Charlotte Joko Beck

From now on
a nameless traveler;
winter's first rain.

Basho

Skillful Guidance

A monk challenged Zhaozhou, "I've been hearing about Zhaozhou's stone bridge for a long time. Now that I'm here, all I see is this log."

Zhaozhou said, "You see the log, but you don't see the stone bridge."

The monk asked, "What is the stone bridge?"

Zhaozhou said, "It lets donkeys cross; it lets horses cross."

○

As a young Zen student, Richard Baker habitually used to come just barely in time for zazen in San Francisco. His teacher Shunryu Suzuki casually said to him once, "You must have many important things to do." After that Baker was never even close to being late.

○

Nanquan was on the mountain working. A monk came by and asked him, "What is the way that leads to Nanquan?" The master raised his sickle and said, "I bought this sickle for thirty cents."

The monk said, "I'm not asking about the sickle you bought for thirty cents. What is the way that leads to Nanquan?"

The master said, "It feels good when I use it."

○

When samadhi develops, we usually introduce a koan. A koan is a nonlogical statement, question, or anecdote, most often an exchange between master and student from the Zen literature. A koan is a means for the student to confront the self, to bypass logical, conceptual thinking. It becomes the object of concentration. This first koan can take many forms. Classically in Zen it would be: What is your original face? The face you had before your parents were born? Show it to me. Or: You know the sound of two hands clapping—what is the sound of one hand clapping? Do not talk about it—show me!

These questions are no different from: What is truth? What is reality? What is life? What is God? Who am I? They are all the same question. They deal with the ultimate nature of reality, the ground of being.

John Daido Loori

Dongshan once taught the assembly, "Concerning realization-through-the-body of going beyond buddha, I would like to talk a little."

A monk said, "What is this talk?"

The master said, "When I talk you don't hear it."

The monk said, "Do you hear it, sir?"

The master said, "Wait till I don't talk, then you hear it."

○

A monk asked, "What is the mind of the ancient buddhas?"

Nanyang said, "Walls, tiles, and pebbles."

The monk said, "Aren't walls, tiles, and pebbles insentient?"

Nanyang said, "That's right."

The monk said, "Then how can they expound the dharma?"

Nanyang said, "They are brilliantly expounding the dharma, constantly and without end."

The monk said "I've never been able to hear it."

Nanyang said, "That you don't hear doesn't mean others can't hear it."

The monk said, "I don't understand. Who hears it?"

Nanyang said, "All the sages do."

○

Zen mind is not Zen mind. That is, if you are attached to Zen mind, then you have a problem, and your way is very narrow. Throwing away Zen mind is correct Zen mind. Only keep the question, "What is the best way of helping other people?"

Seung Sahn

Layman Pang was sitting casually reading a sutra. A monk approached and asked, "Why don't you sit up, and read the sutra properly?"

Layman Pang stood balanced on the toes of one foot.

The monk could say nothing.

○

During an early sesshin with Suzuki Roshi, I was having a very hard time with pain in my legs and back. I went to dokusan and said to him, "When I sit in full lotus, it is very difficult to sit still and concentrate on my breathing. But when I sit in half lotus, my mind is quiet and I am able to sit still and concentrate on my breathing quite easily." Then he suggested, "Why don't you sit in full lotus?"

After we had talked for a while longer, he suddenly said, "Oh, excuse me. I forgot something." He got up from sitting with me and left the room. I could hear him going upstairs to where his office and the meditation hall were located. I could hear him walking down the hall over my head and opening the door to his office. More time passed and I heard the sound of chanting which meant that noon service was going on. During the chanting I noticed that I was quite comfortable. Even though I continued to sit in full lotus, my legs and back were no longer bothering me.

Then I heard the chanting stop and then I heard more chanting start, which meant that lunch was happening. I just sat there while lunch was going on and continued to be amazed by how comfortable I was feeling. Then after about an hour I heard the signals indicating the end of lunch and I could hear people leaving the hall and coming down the stairs and going out for a break. And then some time later I heard the door of Suzuki Roshi's office open and close again, and the sound of him shuffling down the hall and down the stairs, where I had been sitting for over two hours.

He came to the door of the dokusan room, and opened it, came in, saw me and said, "Oh, you are still here!" He sat down facing me. We continued to talk some while longer till we concluded our interview. Still, I was not bothered by the pain. Then I went back to sitting in the zendo. And the pain was there just as before the interview, but it was different.

Tenshin Reb Anderson

Zhaozhou went to a hermitage and called out, "Are you there? Are you there?" The hermit raised his fist.

Zhaozhou commented, "The water is too shallow here to dock a boat," and he left.

Again he went to another hermitage and called out, "Are you there? Are you there?" This hermit also raised his fist.

Zhaozhou said, "You can let go, you can grab, you can kill, and you can let live." Then Zhaozhou made a deep bow.

O

Seung Sahn would say, "When you eat, just eat. When you read the newspaper, just read the newspaper. Don't do anything other than what you are doing."

One day a student saw him reading the newspaper while he was eating. The student asked if this did not contradict his teaching. Seung Sahn said, "When you eat and read the newspaper, just eat and read the newspaper."

O

There were several monks in residence with Hakuin at Shoin-ji. One of the first persons to join the community was a sixteen-year-old girl named Satsu. She was awakened soon after studying with Hakuin. One day she was sitting zazen on a box when her father approached and asked, "What do you think you're doing? Buddha's image is in that box." She replied, "If there is any place where Buddha does not exist, I ask you to take me there." Her father was shocked. On another occasion a monk asked her, "What is the meaning of breaking the white rock within the rubbish heap?" She immediately threw down and shattered the tea bowl she was holding.

On the fourth day of sesshin as we sat with our painful legs, aching backs, hopes and doubts about whether it was worth it, Suzuki Roshi began his talk by slowly saying, "The problems you are now experiencing [*will go away, right?* we were thinking] will ... continue ... for ... the ... rest ... of ... your ... life."

The way he said it, everyone laughed.

Ed Brown

A monk asked Dongshan, "When cold or heat comes, how can we avoid them?"

Dongshan said, "Why not go where there is no cold or heat?"

The monk said, "What do you mean by 'where there is no cold or heat'?"

Dongshan said, "When it's cold, cold kills you; when it's hot, heat kills you."

When Nyogen was dismissed from his job as houseboy—he worked hard but was inexperienced and spoke no English—Soyen Shaku escorted him toward a Japanese hotel in San Francisco. While walking through Golden Gate Park, the master came to an abrupt halt, saying, "This may be better for you instead of being hampered as my attendant monk. Just face this great city and see whether it conquers you or you conquer it." Taking his leave, he walked away into the evening; his disciple never saw him again.

○

A student asked Soen Nakagawa during a meditation retreat, "I am very discouraged. What should I do?"

Soen replied, "Encourage others."

Just Sitting

When I was in China in a Zen monastery, one time I was reading the sayings of an ancient master. A monk from Szechwan asked me, "What's the use of that?"

I said, "When I go home, I want to guide people."

The monk asked, "What's the use of that?"

I said, "For benefiting sentient beings."

The monk said, "In the end, what's the use of that?"

Later I thought about this conversation, and realized that studying the sayings and stories of ancient masters and expounding them for deluded people is of no use in awakening ourselves and guiding others.

If you just sit, clarify the great matter, and understand the essence, the power of this is boundless in awakening others, even without reading one word. I think that is why the monk said, "In the end, what's the use of that?" Afterward I stopped reading the recorded sayings of old masters, and just sat.

Dogen

Zen is a teaching about how we can sit with stillness in the midst of our self, our heart, our breath and the world, and then to let them open into our wider self and into the world of other people. In this mind, the world passes transparently through us and we start to feel how there is neither outside nor inside. Everyday this practice touches more and more of our life, and we come to know what the koans and sutras are talking about.

Richard Baker

Zhaozhou asked Nanquan, "What is the way?"

Nanquan said, "Ordinary mind is the way."

Zhaozhou asked, "Shall I try for that?"

Nanquan said, "If you try you'll miss it."

Zhaozhou asked, "How do I know it's the way if I don't try?"

Nanquan said, "The way has nothing to do with knowing or not knowing. Knowing is illusion; not knowing is ignorance. If you penetrate the way of no-trying, it will be wide open—empty and vast. What need is there to affirm this or deny it?"

Zhaozhou was suddenly enlightened upon hearing this.

○

ON ZAZEN PRACTICE

The moon
abiding in the midst of
serene mind;
billows break
into light.

Dogen

If there is no clear awareness of how this human mind and body functions from moment to moment, division and conflict continue and compound. Having an image of oneself and of what one should do or should not do creates duality and has nothing to do with undivided attention to what actually is taking place.

Attention comes from nowhere. It has no cause. It belongs to no one. When it functions effortlessly, there is no duality.

Toni Packer

Now, all ancestors and all buddhas who unfold buddha-dharma have made it the true path of enlightenment to sit upright practicing in the midst of self-fulfilling samadhi. Those who attained enlightenment in India and China followed this way. It was done so because teachers and disciples personally transmitted this excellent method as the essence of the teaching.

In the authentic tradition of our teaching, it is said that this directly transmitted, straightforward buddha-dharma is the unsurpassable of the unsurpassable. From the first time you meet a master, without engaging in incense offering, bowing, chanting Buddha's name, repentance, or reading scriptures, you should just wholeheartedly sit, and thus drop away body and mind.

Dogen

At dawn sitting, I imagine myself a deer in the early woods. The hard autumn bell note of a blue jay tingles the hairs of the deer's dew-silvered hide, its steps are crisp and sure yet soundless in the leaves. Such images help concentrate my breathing, make me taut and aware. Later they will fall away like armatures, like scaffolding, I will not need them. At dokusan, I ask Soen Roshi if it is all right to use such devices, or should I struggle to empty out my mind? He says it is all right: "There is no such thing as 'empty mind.' There is only *present* mind."

Peter Matthiessen

Be soft in your practice. Think of the method as a fine silvery stream, not a raging waterfall. Follow the stream, have faith in its course. It will go its own way, meandering here, trickling there. It will find the grooves, the cracks, the crevices. Just follow it. Never let it out of your sight. It will take you.

Sheng-yen

The notion that the koan or breath counting are devices or techniques can be misleading. The term *upaya*, "skillful means," is very useful in our practice, but it too can be deceptive. The idea that once you reach the other shore the raft can be discarded is ultimately not true. The raft *is* the shore. Your koan, each point in your breath-counting sequence, your inhalation, then your exhalation—there is the shore itself.

Robert Aitken

For half a year just having rice and sitting on Wan Peak.
This sitting cuts off misty clouds, thousands of layers.
Suddenly the sound of roaring thunder.
Sacred village's spring activity—apricot blossoms are
    red.

Rujing

A gentle rain settles the dust.
A cool refreshing breeze cleans the air.
Breath absorbed in breath.
The ancient sand castles are nowhere to be found.

Ed Brown

In this world of dreams,
dozing off still more;
and again speaking
and dreaming of dreams.
Just let it be.

Ryokan

If you're afraid of being grabbed by God, don't look at
a wall.
Definitely don't sit still.

Jiyu Kennett

Meditating deeply upon dharma,
reach the depth of the source.
Branching streams cannot compare to this source!
Sitting alone in a great silence
Even though the heavens turn and the earth is upset,
You will not even wink.

Nyogen Senzaki

Now I would like to talk about our zazen posture. When you sit in the full lotus position, your left foot is on your right thigh, and your right foot is on your left thigh. When we cross our legs like this, even though we have a right leg and a left leg, they have become one. The position expresses the oneness of duality: not two, and not one. This is the most important teaching: not two, and not one. Our body and mind are not two and not one. If you think your body and mind are two, that is wrong; if you think that they are one, that is also wrong. Our body and mind are both two *and* one. We usually think that if something is not one, it is more than one; if it is not singular, it is plural. But in actual experience, our life is not only plural, but also singular. Each one of us is both dependent and independent.

After some years we will die. If we just think that it is the end of our life, this will be the wrong understanding. But, on the other hand, if we think that we do not die, this is also wrong. We die, and we do not die. This is the right understanding. Some people may say that our mind or soul exists forever, and it is only our physical body which dies. But this is not exactly right, because both mind and body have their end. But at the same time it is also true that they exist eternally. And even though we say mind and body, they are actually two sides of one coin. This is the right understanding. So when we take this posture it symbolizes this truth. When I have the left foot on the right side of my body, and the right foot on the left side of my body, I do not know which is which. So either may be the left or the right side.

The most important thing in taking the zazen posture is to keep your spine straight. Your ears and your shoulders should be on one line. Relax your shoulders, and push up towards the ceiling with the back of your head. And you should pull your chin in. When your chin is tilted up, you have no strength in your posture; you are probably dreaming. Also to gain strength in your posture, press your diaphragm down towards your *hara*, or lower abdomen. This will help you maintain your physical and mental balance. When you try to keep this posture, at first you may find some difficulty breathing naturally, but when you get accustomed to it you will be able to breathe naturally and deeply.

Your hands should form the "cosmic mudra." If you put your left hand on top of your right, middle joints of your middle fingers together, and touch your thumbs lightly together (as if you held a piece of paper between them), your hands will make a beautiful oval. You should keep this universal mudra with great care, as if you were holding something precious in your hand. Your hands should be held against your body, with your thumbs at about the height of your navel. Hold your arms freely and easily, and slightly away from your body, as if you held an egg under each arm without breaking it.

You should not be tilted sideways, backwards, or forwards. You should be sitting straight up as if you were supporting the sky with your head. This is not just form or breathing. It expresses the key point of Buddhism. It is a perfect expression of your Buddha nature. If you want true understanding of Buddhism, you should practice this way. These forms are not a means of obtaining the right state of mind. To take this posture itself is the purpose of our practice. When you have this posture, you have the right state of mind, so there is no need to try to attain some special state. When you try to attain something, your mind starts to wander about somewhere else. When you do not try to attain anything, you have your own body and mind right here. A Zen master would say, "Kill the Buddha!" Kill the Buddha if the Buddha exists somewhere else. Kill the Buddha, because you should resume your own Buddha nature.

Doing something is expressing our own nature. We do not exist for the sake of something else. We exist for the sake of ourselves. This is the fundamental teaching expressed in the forms we observe. Just as for sitting, when we stand in the zendo we have some rules. But the purpose of these rules is not to make everyone the same, but to allow each to express his own self most freely. For instance, each one of us has his own way of standing, so our standing posture is based on the proportions of our own bodies. When you stand, your heels should be as far apart as the width of your own fist, your big toes in line with the centers of your breasts. As in zazen, put some strength in your abdomen. Here also your hands should express your self. Hold your left hand against your chest with fingers encircling your thumb, and put your right hand over it. Holding your thumb pointing downward, and your forearms parallel to the floor, you feel as if you have some round pillar in your grasp—a big round temple pillar—so you cannot be slumped or tilted to the side.

The most important point is to own your own physical body. If you slump, you will lose your self. Your mind will be wandering about somewhere else; you will not be in your body. This is not the way. We must exist right here, right now! This is the key point. You must have your own body and mind. Everything should exist in the right place, in the right way. Then there is no problem. If the microphone I use when I speak exists somewhere else, it will not serve its purpose. When we have our body and mind in order, everything else will exist in the right place, in the right way.

But usually, without being aware of it, we try to change something other than ourselves, we try to order things outside us. But it is impossible to organize things if you yourself are not in order. When you do things in the right way, at the right time, everything else will be organized. You are the "boss." When the boss is sleeping, everything is sleeping. When the boss does something right, everyone will do everything right, and at the right time. That is the secret of Buddhism.

So try always to keep the right posture, not only when you practice zazen, but in all your activities. Take the right posture when you are driving your car, and when you are reading. If you read in a slumped position, you cannot stay awake long. Try. You will discover how important it is to keep the right posture. This is the true teaching. The teaching which is written on paper is not the true teaching. Written teaching is a kind of food for your brain. Of course it is necessary to take some food for your brain, but it is more important to be yourself by practicing the right way of life.

That is why Buddha could not accept the religions existing at his time. He studied many religions, but he was not satisfied with their practices. He could not find the answer in asceticism or in philosophies. He was not interested in some metaphysical existence, but in his own body and mind, here and now. And when he found himself, he found that everything that exists has Buddha nature. That was his enlightenment. Enlightenment is not some good feeling or some particular state of mind. The state of mind that exists when you sit in the right posture is, itself, enlightenment. If you cannot be satisfied with the state of mind you have in zazen, it means your mind is still wandering about. Our body and mind should not be wobbling or wandering about. In this posture there is no need to talk about the right state of mind. You already have it. This is the conclusion of Buddhism.

Shunryu Suzuki

Inside the zendo also
dancing
evening maple leaves

Soen Nakagawa

Chopping Wood

It is hard to even begin to gauge how much a complication of possessions, the notions of "my and mine," stand between us and a true, clear, liberated way of seeing the world. To live lightly on the earth, to be aware and alive, to be free of egotism, to be in contact with plants and animals, starts with simple concrete acts. The inner principle is the insight that we are interdependent energy-fields of great potential wisdom and compassion—expressed in each person as a superb mind, a handsome and complex body, and the almost magical capacity of language. To these potentials and capacities, "owning things" can add nothing of authenticity. "Clad in the sky, with the earth for a pillow."

Gary Snyder

While thinking about the future, and about tomorrow's livelihood, if you don't let go of worldly affairs, if you don't practice the Way, and if you pass your days and nights in vain, you'll regret it. You should rouse your mind, and determine that even if there is no livelihood for tomorrow, and you might freeze, or starve, or even die—still today, you should hear the Way, and follow Buddha's intention. If you do this, you will certainly achieve practice of the Way.

Dogen

A woman was pouring tea for guests in the kitchen at Plum Village, France. The tea cups were straightly arrayed on the tray and the amount of tea in each cup was exactly the same, as she had been trained in a Japanese-style Zen Center in the United States. Thich Nhat Hanh walked by and saw what she was doing. Smiling at her, he put his finger in one cup after another.

○

Either hoeing the garden
or washing bottles at the well,
making soup for a sick man
or listening to someone else's child,
studying books, stacking logs,
writing to the local paper
or pulling that stubborn lamb
into our world, I hear
the song which carries my neighbor
from one thing to the next:
Earth feeds us
out of her empty bowl

Peter Levitt

Our goals in this practice of nonattainment may be quite modest—to be present in each moment's sensation, perception, feeling, thought. We stop looking for some other moment.

It is wonderful to explore and continue turning the question of "who am I?" or "what is this life?" so that we are simply open to what it means to be alive—to be in a body. And if we really don't know, which we don't, then the searching, the wandering, the questioning, the never-arriving, is a wonderfully liberating way to live.

Katherine Thanas

Zen monastery
unpretentiously
prepared for winter

The preparation may almost look nonchalant. Everything that needs to be attended to is done, yet no trace of effort is apparent. This poem describes the spirit of my master, Gempo Yamamoto Roshi, who was spending most of his time doing zazen. And often he was completely absorbed in studying the Diamond Sutra. He would say that you are not yet mature if you are seen as great or wise by other people. It is not good to be absent-minded, but you should be fully unpretentious while you are aware of all necessary matters. This is important.

Soen Nakagawa

For a Zen student real freedom means laying down the burden of partiality, the enslavement to our thoughts, feelings and emotions, as well as the desire for security in material things. The point of our practice is to be able to unburden ourselves and return to reality moment by moment. It is not necessary to know everything. Renunciation is simply choosing to wake up moment by moment.

Life is constantly giving us our cues. When the bell sounds, the monks put on their robes and go to the meditation hall. When anger arises, the bell sounds and we take refuge in calmness of mind. When confusion arises, the bell sounds and we take refuge in equanimity. When greed arises, the bell sounds and we take refuge in the coolness of appreciating what we already have. In this way, everything in our life is helping and supporting our practice. I make a bow with deep appreciation.

Sojun Mel Weitsman

What a laugh!
That actor just now
Serving tea in the zendo
Thinks he's me!

Lou Hartman

I've built a grass hut where there's nothing of value.
After eating, I relax and enjoy a nap.
When it was completed, fresh weeds appeared.
Now it's been lived in—covered by weeds.
The person in the hut lives here calmly,
not stuck to inside, outside, or in between.
Places worldly people live, he doesn't live.
Realms worldly people love, he doesn't love.
Though the hut is small, it includes the entire world.
In ten square feet, an old man illumines forms and
     their nature.
A Great Vehicle bodhisattva trusts without doubt.
The middling or lowly can't help wondering;
Will this hut perish or not?
Perishable or not, the original master is present,
not dwelling south or north, east or west.
Firmly based on steadiness, it can't be surpassed.
A shining window below the green pines—
jade palaces or vermilion towers can't compare with it.
Just sitting with head covered, all things are at rest.
Thus, this mountain monk doesn't understand at all.
Living here he no longer works to get free.
Who would proudly arrange seats, trying to entice
     guests?
Turn around the light to shine within, then just return.
The vast inconceivable source can't be faced or turned
     away from.
Meet the ancestral teachers, be familiar with their
     instruction,
bind grasses to build a hut, and don't give up.

Let go of hundreds of years and relax completely.
Open your hands and walk, innocent.
Thousands of words, myriad interpretations,
are only to free you from obstructions.
If you want to know the undying person in the hut,
don't separate from this skin bag here and now.

Shitou

In this assembly, no one is absent and no one is ignorant. This is a gathering of the Buddha-mind that is given to us at birth. When you return home, be mindful of all your daily matters, just the way you are listening to the teachings now. Then you'll be just living with unborn Buddha-mind. Because of desire, we become stubborn, self-centered, and deluded. This way we move away from Buddha-mind, and become foolish. Originally, no one is deluded.

Bankei

If you saw an avoidance type and a seeking type sweeping leaves, you probably wouldn't notice any difference in their appearance—but their attitudes wouldn't be the same. The seeking type would be thinking, maybe, something like, "Oh boy, I'm deep into Zen now. This was Han Shan's practice—sweep the ground, sweep your mind. Any moment now I might be struck by the Great Enlightenment. Then the master will recognize me and I'll be known by all as a great teacher and thousands will flock to hear my talks and . . ."

The avoidance type might be thinking something more like, "Oh well, I can't get out of this, I guess. Hmm, sure would be nice to walk down that valley, in and out of the oak and bamboo groves, walk by the paddies' edges, watch the birds and the butterflies, maybe go down to the falls . . ."

In that spirit, one day during work, I raked myself off from the others and, putting a leaf in a runoff trough, followed it as it emptied into a larger trough and then a ditch. The leaf floated across and down the hillside, around bends and over miniature waterfalls all the way to the creek. Before I knew it I'd gotten myself far down the hill and had to hightail it back before they put out an all-points bulletin on me.

Often the seeker and the avoider are at odds with each other. Sometimes they even divide into cliques that roam monastic halls. It could be said that the avoiders are seeking and that the seekers are avoiding. They're merely different expressions of the age-old near-impossibility of just being.

David Chadwick

Americans like to refer to one of the old Zen stories about how a master took a wooden Buddha image, chopped it up, and made a fire, warming himself by its flames. Seeing this, a monk asked, "What are you doing, setting fire to the Buddha?"

The master replied, "Where is Buddha?"

The opposite goes on in America. In America we want to burn the Buddha images to begin with. You see, that monk was stuck in the image, stuck on the form. In America, we are antiform, so the pointing goes in another direction. If you're attached to neither existence nor nonexistence, you manifest a sixteen-foot golden Buddha in a pile of shit and rubbish, appearing and disappearing.

John Daido Loori

Lilacs—peeling stucco—vines
I take out garbage
Old cans and bottles to the curb

I pack my daughter's lunch
In the pink lunch box
Not sure

If these actions are mundane
Or part of the endless
Preservation of the world

Zen teacher Ikkyu
Is under the bridge again
With bag ladies and the girls in spandex

I don't know
If I should invite him home
Or leave my key in the mailbox
And move in with him.

Miriam Sagan

A moment's absence—
a dead person.

Yantou

Cloud Water Assembly

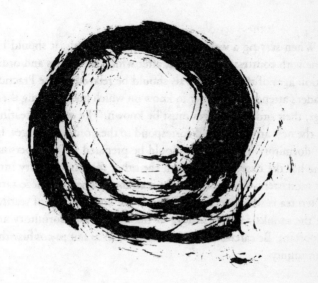

Monastery gate
huge wooden bolt
fragrant wind

Mitsu Suzuki

When serving a welcoming tea for new arrivals, it should be done with courtesy and respect, after which the names and ordination ages of the new arrivals should be relayed by the Practice Leader's attendant. In order to know on which hook to hang their bags, their ordination ages must be known. The order of seating for the new arrivals should correspond to their ordination ages. In the dormitory, two plaques should be prepared for each person. One has the date of ordination, the other the date of entry into the monastery. These plaques are rearranged when it is necessary. When tea is served in the dormitory, the arrangement of seating for the monks and the seating of the head of the dormitory are important. Be careful to do this correctly so as not to confuse the community.

Dogen

TEMPLE RULES: ON KEEPING
THE BODHI MIND

You must first make a firm decision to attain enlightenment and help others. You already have the five or the ten precepts. Know when to keep them and when to break them, when they are open and when they are closed. Let go of your small self and become your true self.

> In original nature
> There is no this and that.
> The Great Round Mirror
> Has no likes or dislikes.

Seung Sahn

A THOUSAND PROSTRATIONS

Palms together and bow at the waist,
follow gravity down to the knees
and forward, till forehead touches floor,
palms lifted above the ears, lowered,
then slowly rise. Outside warblers call.
Sunlight dims and brightens in dusty
blocks across the hardwood floor; forehead
warms with contact, cooling as you stand.
More than just continuing until
the difference between warm and cool makes
no difference, or until you forget
how far you've counted, that you're counting,
even that you're bowing: going on
till you're bowing even when you're not.

Allen Hoey

The essence of the Monastery Director's work is to revere the wise and include the many, being harmonious to the seniors and friendly with the juniors. The Director should give comfort to the community of monks who share the same practice, and let them have a joyful mind. He should not depend upon his power or authority and belittle the members of the community. He should not carry out things willfully and make the members of the community insecure. When he is not sick or meeting with government officials, he should follow the zendo schedule. The value of this monastic arrangement is that it enables the Director as well as the workers in the kitchen to share the same practice. If the stock in the storehouse falls short, the Director should do his best to solve the problem. In a case like this, he shouldn't overburden the Abbot or broadcast to the community.

Dogen

I had only been given the opportunity to serve food in the zendo once the year before and in a spectacular display of one-pointedness and "just do it" mind had served an entire ladleful of yogurt into the gaping sleeve of a fellow practitioner's robe as she waited, hands in gassho, for her yummy dessert. Not one drop made it into the bowl. This time I was determined to do better.

And so far I was. I was practically through with my round of the zendo, serving the waiting sesshin participants from the hefty and slightly unwieldy ten-quart pot of soup. I had managed to maintain a sushi menu of procedure to help me avoid the previous year's mistake: Footsteps. Stop. Bow. Kneel. Serve. Aware. Elegant. Rise. Bow. Footsteps. Etc. Etc. One after another, it was going well.

As I reached the next to last row needing service I felt something ever so slight in the area of my *hara*. Or just below. Yes, it was my sitting pants, the nice, big, *oversized* ones I had bought specially to wear beneath my robes so I could be comfortable sitting so much during sesshin. I felt these pants begin to slide just a little down onto my hips and I realized the drawstring must have somehow come undone. Holding my big pot of soup just above nose level I took a step forward and felt, to my horror, my pants continue to slide further down until they rested halfway on my hips. An army of sweat began to march across my forehead, very inelegant, and as I took a step toward the next pair of students to serve I felt my pants start to really let loose beneath my robes.

Quickly I stuck one leg out to catch them before they hit the floor and as I did this the head-high ten-quart soup pot lurched in the opposite direction with a slosh. I was now standing like a hobbled crane before my waiting fellow students whose hands were in gassho and whose large black sleeves gaped at me in awe. Or so they seemed. I bowed (briefly), somehow knelt, served, stood almost completely up, bowed again and tried to take a step toward the next pair. As I did this my secret inched onto my thighs, ever closer toward revelation, and I stuck one hip and leg out to catch the slide. With one knee turned in, one pointed out, ankles snowplowing and butt striking the oddest pose I hobbled forward like a very poor student of the latest Brazilian dance. And with this motion my pants slid to my knees, where I realized not another step would be allowed. Form is form. And I realized I was now standing in front of the roshi's wife.

Good news? Bad news? It didn't matter. Finally the teachings were beginning to sink in. I made the briefest gassho with my pot, a nod really, and then with terror and exhilaration stood straight up and let my pants reach their destiny. The softest sound in the world. I knelt, placed my pot on the floor, gasshoed, opened my robes, slid my errant trousers back up to my waist, tied the naughty cord *tight,* reassembled my robes, gasshoed one more time to the kind, kind person before me (she did not budge the entire time) and, with a different kind of confidence, began to serve.

Peter Levitt

Dusk surrounds the canyon
the wooden mallet's clack
signals zazen

Mitsu Suzuki

SAYINGS OF A ZEN MASTER

1. Don't wish for perfect health. In perfect health there is greed and wanting. So an ancient said, "Make good medicine from the suffering of sickness."

2. Don't hope for a life without problems. An easy life results in a judgmental and lazy mind. So an ancient once said, "Accept the anxieties and difficulties of this life."

3. Don't expect your practice to be always clear of obstacles. Without hindrances the mind that seeks enlightenment may be burnt out. So an ancient once said, "Attain deliverance in disturbances."

4. Don't expect to practice hard and not experience the weird. Hard practice that evades the unknown makes for a weak commitment. So an ancient once said, "Help hard practice by befriending every demon."

5. Don't expect to finish doing something easily. If you happen to acquire something easily the will is made weaker. So an ancient once said, "Try again and again to complete what you are doing."

6. Make friends but don't expect any benefit for yourself. Friendship only for oneself harms trust. So an ancient once said, "Have an enduring friendship with purity in heart."

7. Don't expect others to follow your direction. When it happens that others go along with you, it results in pride. So an ancient once said, "Use your will to bring peace between people."

8. Expect no reward for an act of charity. Expecting something in return leads to a scheming mind. So an ancient once said, "Throw false spirituality away like a pair of old shoes."

9. Don't seek profit over and above what your work is worth. Acquiring false profit makes a fool (of oneself). So an ancient once said, "Be rich in honesty."

10. Don't try to make clarity of mind with severe practice. Every mind comes to hate severity, and where is clarity in mortification? So an ancient once said, "Clear a passageway through severe practice."

11. Be equal to every hindrance. Buddha attained supreme enlightenment without hindrance. Seekers after truth are schooled in adversity. When they are confronted by a hindrance, they can't be overcome. Then, cutting free, their treasure is great.

Kyong Ho

Yaoshan was an ancient buddha. His community was less than ten monks. Zhaozhou was also an ancient buddha, and his community was less than twenty monks. Feyang only had seven or eight students. Buddha ancestors, great dragons, were not limited by the number of monks they had. Just revere those who have the Way, without seeking an abundance of students in the community.

Dogen

Dongshan asked a monk, "What's the most painful thing in this world?"

The monk said, "Hell is the most painful."

Dongshan said, "Not so. If you wear monk's robes, and underneath, you have not clarified the great matter, that's the most painful thing."

○

"Harada talked a lot about listening," Tetsugen told me as we walked in the court garden at Hosshin-ji. "How when you go to teisho, you should be the only listener in the room. If there is just you and the teacher, you will listen: otherwise, you tend to give responsibility to others. And as you listen, doing zazen, there will no longer be two people in the room, no subject and object, just the One. And that is the way to read Dogen Zenji, too."

Peter Matthiessen

SHAKYAMUNI'S AUSTERITIES

Six years of starving, and being frozen to the bone.
Asceticism is the dark mystery of Buddha ancestors.
Believe me, no one is born a Shakyamuni.
Monks all over are just rice bags.

Ikkyu

DECEMBER

Three a.m.—a far bell
   coming closer:
fling up useless futon on the shelf;
outside, ice-water in the hand & wash the face.
   Ko the bird-head, silent, skinny,
    swiftly cruise the room with
    salt plum tea.

Bell from the hondo chanting sutras. Gi:
deep bell, small bell, wooden drum.
   sanzen at four
   kneel on icy polisht boards in line:

Shukuza rice and pickles
barrel and bucket
dim watt bulb.
   till daybreak nap upright.
         sweep

garden and hall.
frost outside
                    wind through walls

At eight the lecture bell.   high chair.
Ke helps the robe—red, gold,
    black lacquer in the shadow
    sun and cold

Saiza a quarter to ten
soup and rice dab on the bench
feed the hungry ghosts
    back in the hall by noon.
two o clock sanzen
three o clock bellywarmer
    boild up soup-rice mush.
dinging and scuffing.   out back smoke,
                    and talk.

At dusk, at five,
black robes draw into the hall.
    stiff joints, sore knees bend
    the jiki pads by with his incense lit,
                        bells,
    wood block crack
& stick slips round the room
on soft straw sandals.

seven, sanzen
tea, and a leaf-shaped candy.
kinhin at eight with folden hands—
    single-file racing in flying robes leaning
                    to wake—

nine o clock one more sanzen
ten, hot noodles,
three bowls each.

Sit until midnight.   chant.
    make three bows and pull the futon down.
    roll in the bed—
    black.

A far bell coming closer

Gary Snyder

   As you like Zen Center so much, you will easily be involved in
a kind of self-centered idea. To think about only yourself is a self-
centered idea, of course; but to think only about Zen Center is a
kind of small mind. Zen Center is just a small speck of dust com-
pared with big buddha land. As Dogen Zenji says in his *"Fukan-
zazengi"*: "If your purpose in zazen misses the point just a little
bit, then the separation will be as great as heaven and earth."
Then our zazen will not make any sense. We should be able to
give up Zen Center when it is not necessary.

Shunryu Suzuki

How to Cook Enlightenment

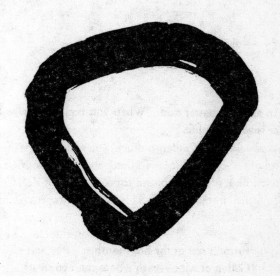

Dongshan asked Yunju, "What are you doing?"
Yunju said, "I'm making soy paste."
Dongshan said, " Are you using some salt?"
Yunju said, "I turn some in."
Dongshan asked "How does it taste?"
Yunju said, "Done."

○

An ancient master said, "When you boil rice, know that the water is your own life."

○

Farmers rest in the hot month.
Gallon of wine—with whom can I enjoy it?
A cluttered array of mountain nuts . . .
bare space around the wine jar.
Rushes serve for my mats,
plantain leaves, for now, my plates.
After drinking I sit holding my chin—
Mount Sumeru—just a pellet!

Hanshan

Xuefeng was once tenzo at the monastery of Dongshan Liangjie. One day when Xuefeng was washing rice, Dongshan asked him, "Do you wash the sand away from the rice or the rice away from the sand?"

Xuefeng replied, "I wash both sand and rice away at the same time."

"What will the assembly eat?" said Dongshan. Xuefeng covered the rice-washing bowl.

Dongshan said, "You will probably meet a true person some day."

○

Watermelons and Zen students
grow pretty much the same way.
Long periods of sitting
till they ripen and grow
all juicy inside, but
when you knock them on the head
to see if they're ready—
sounds like nothing's going on.

Peter Levitt

When preparing vegetables or soup, don't worry—just prepare them with sincerity. Most of all, try to avoid getting upset or complaining about the quantity or quality of the food. Practice in such a way that things come and abide in your mind, and your mind returns and abides in things, all through the day and night.

Dogen

During dinner one night at San Francisco Zen Center someone asked, "How do you cook enlightenment?"

A young woman said, "Over easy."

○

Zhaozhou asked a newly arrived monk, "Have you been here before?"

The monk said, "Yes I have been here."

Zhaozhou said, "Have some tea."

Again, he asked another monk, "Have you been here before?"

The monk said, "No, I haven't been here."

The master said, "Have some tea."

The temple director then asked the master, "Why do you say, 'Have some tea,' to someone who has been here, and 'Have some tea,' to someone who has not?"

The master said, "Director." When the director responded, the master said, "Have some tea."

○

During my stay at Mt. Tiantong, a priest named Yong from Qingyuan Prefecture held the position of tenzo. One day after the noon meal when I was walking along the eastern covered walkway to a sub-temple called Chaoran Hut, he was in front of the buddha hall drying some mushrooms in the sun. He had a bamboo stick in his hand and no hat on his head. The sun was very hot, scorching the pavement. It looked very painful; his backbone was bent like a bow and his eyebrows were as white as a crane.

I went up to the tenzo and asked, "How long have you been a monk?"

"Sixty-eight years," he replied.

"Why don't you let a helper do it?"

"Others are not myself."

"Reverend sir, you follow regulations exactly, but as the sun is so hot why do you work so hard as this?"

"Until when should I wait?"

So I stopped talking. As I was walking further along the covered walkway, I thought about how important the tenzo's position is.

Dogen

Someone once asked Issan, "Tenzo! We are vegetarians, so we don't kill animals. But we eat carrots and potatoes. What do you think about killing vegetables?"

Issan replied, "Well, I definitely think we should kill them before we eat them."

○

The ingredients have their own boundless virtue—which is your virtue too. That is the Zen spirit.

Ed Brown

To turn things while being turned by things, keep yourself harmonious and wholehearted, and don't lose an eye, or two eyes. Taking up a green vegetable, turn it into a 16-foot golden body; take a 16-foot golden body and turn it into a green vegetable. This is miraculous transformation—a work of buddha that benefits sentient beings.

Dogen

Daily Reminders

At the foot of the Bodhi tree,
beautifully seated, peaceful and smiling,
the living source of understanding and compassion,
to the Buddha I go for refuge.

The path of mindful living,
leading to healing, joy, and enlightenment,
the way of peace,
to the Dharma I go for refuge.

The loving and supportive community of practice,
realizing harmony, awareness, and liberation,
to the Sangha I go for refuge.

I am aware that the Three Gems are within my heart.
I vow to realize them.
I vow to practice mindful breathing and smiling,
looking deeply into things.
I vow to understand living beings and their suffering,
to cultivate compassion and loving kindness,
and to practice joy and equanimity.

I vow to offer joy to one person in the morning
and to help relieve the grief of one person in the afternoon.
I vow to live simply and sanely,
content with just a few possessions,
and to keep my body healthy.
I vow to let go of all worry and anxiety in order to be light
    and free.

I am aware that I owe so much to my parents, teachers,
    friends, and all beings.
I vow to be worthy of their trust,

to practice wholeheartedly,
so that understanding and compassion will flower,
and I can help living beings
be free from their suffering.

May the Buddha, the Dharma, and the Sangha support my
   efforts.

Thich Nhat Hanh

ONE AND MANY ENGAGED

The Great Sage of India transmitted his realization
directly east and west.
Although there are differences in personality
the way goes beyond southern or northern ancestors.

The wondrous source shines brightly.
Its branches spread in darkness.
Attachment to things is delusion.
Knowing this essence is not yet enlightenment.

All objects in each sense-field
merge yet don't merge with one another.
When they merge, they embrace all things.
Otherwise they maintain their own place.

Forms vary in shape.
Sounds vary in tone.
Darkness blends higher and lower.
Brightness separates clear and murky.

The four great elements have their own nature
just as a child its mother:
fire heats, air moves,
water wets, earth is solid.

Eyes perceive forms, ears perceive sound,
a nose responds to odors, a tongue to taste.
The root of each function
generates branches and leaves.

A river and its tributaries
return to ocean.
Both true and false are expressed through words.
Right in brightness there is darkness.
Don't treat it as mere darkness.

Right in darkness there is brightness.
Don't regard it as mere brightness.
Brightness and darkness anticipate each other
just as one foot follows the other.

Things in themselves have virtue.
Name them according to how and where they work.
When things are as they are, the lid fits the box.
Realizing essence is like arrowheads meeting in mid-air.

When it comes to words
you must understand their true meaning.
Don't set up arbitrary standards.

If you don't see the path that meets your eye
how will your feet know the way?
Moving forward isn't a question of near or far.
When you are lost, mountains and rivers block your way.

Please let me remind you
who study the inconceivable:
Your time is running fast.
Don't ignore it.

Shitou

SONG OF THE BRIGHT MIRROR
SAMADHI

This dharma as it is has been directly entrusted
by buddha ancestors.
Now that you have realized it
you must guard it mindfully.

Snow heaped in a silver bowl,
a heron fading into the bright moon.
Similar but unequal.
Place them side by side and you will see which is which.

The meaning is not in words.
Inquiring students seek further.
Moving forward creates pitfalls.
Avoidance leads to a standstill.

Faced with a great wall of fire,
turning your back on it and touching it are both wrong.
Expressing it in colorful words
only stains it.

Midnight is bright,
dawn brings no dew.
Things are truth itself
to be used for removing delusion.
This is not created
and yet not inexpressible.

As form and image face each other
in a bright mirror,
you are not it
but it is you.

It is like a baby
perfectly possessing five freedoms:
Not coming, not going,
not rising, not staying . . .

And goo goo wa wa—
words that are not words.
In the end nothing is grasped
because speech is not precise.

In the double-split hexagrams
the particular and the general integrate.
When the lines are closed they become three,
and its final change makes five.

A blade of *zhi* grass has five flavors,
A vajra has five points.
Within the general, something marvelous lies.
Drumming and singing go together.

Penetrating the source, penetrating the paths.
Here is a short path, here is a long path.
If you miss it, that's a good sign.
Don't neglect it.

What is natural and inconceivable
belongs neither to delusion nor enlightenment.
Causes and conditions right at this moment
shine completely in the silence.

So minute that it penetrates any space.
So enormous that it exceeds all bounds.
The slightest difference
puts it out of tune.

Because the basic teachings of sudden and gradual
have been set up,
the Zen school has become divided.
These ways have become standard.
Even though you master such teachings
the truth keeps on escaping.

You may sit still but waver inside—
a tied-up horse, or a cowering rat.
The Ancient Teacher pitied us
and transmitted the dharma.

Because of our delusions
we say black is white.
When delusions disappear
understanding reveals itself.

If you wish to conform to the old ways,
take a lesson from the past.
People trying to attain the buddha way
by gazing for ten eons at a tree
are like a tiger with tattered ears
or a hobbled horse.

A greedy mind sees
rare treasures.
A surprised mind sees
raccoons and white bulls.

Legendary bowman Yi with his skill
shoots the mark a hundred paces away.
When arrowheads meet head-on,
is it only a matter of skill?

Right when a wooden man sings
a stone woman gets up and dances.
It's not within the reach of knowledge
nor does it admit ideas.

Retainers serve their lord;
children obey their father.
Without obedience there is no respect;
without service there is no civic virtue.

Conceal your practice, work inside.
Be ignorant, look foolish.
Just keep on doing it.
This is called host with host.

Dongshan

IN PRAISE OF ZAZEN

Sentient beings are in essence buddhas.
It is like water and ice.
There is no ice without water,
there are no buddhas outside sentient beings.

What a shame, sentient beings seek afar,
not knowing what is at hand.
It is like wailing from thirst
in the midst of water,
or wandering lost among the poor,
although born a rich man's child.

The cause of rebirth in the six realms
is the darkness of our delusion.
Treading dark path after dark path
when can we escape birth and death?

Mahayana Zen meditation
goes beyond all praise.
Giving, keeping precepts, and the other perfections,
chanting Buddha's name, repentance, training and
many other kinds of wholesome deeds
all find their source in zazen.

When you sit even once,
the merit obliterates countless wrongdoings.
How can there be evil realms?
The Pure Land is not far.

If by good fortune you have the occasion
to hear this teaching,
admire it and rejoice in it.

You will attain boundless happiness—
how much more if you dedicate yourself
and realize your own nature directly.

This own-nature is no nature.
You are already apart from useless discussions.
The gate opens where cause and effect are inseparable,
The road of not-two, not-three goes straight ahead.

Make the form formless form,
going and returning, not anywhere else.
Make the thought thoughtless thought,
singing and dancing, the dharma voice.

How vast the sky of unobstructed concentration!
How brilliant the full moon of fourfold wisdom!

At this very moment, what can be sought?
Nirvana is immediate.
This place is the lotus land.
This body is the buddha body.

Hakuin

The Bodhisattva Avalokita, while moving in the deep course of Perfect Understanding, shed light on the five skandhas and found them equally empty. After this penetration, he overcame all pain.

"Listen, Shariputra, form is emptiness, emptiness is form, form does not differ from emptiness, emptiness does not differ from form. The same is true with feelings, perceptions, mental formations, and consciousness.

"Hear, Shariputra, all dharmas are marked with emptiness; they are neither produced nor destroyed, neither defiled nor immaculate, neither increasing nor decreasing. Therefore, in emptiness there is neither form, nor feeling, nor perception, nor mental formations, nor consciousness; no eye, or ear, or nose, or tongue, or body, or mind, no form, no sound, no smell, no taste, no touch, no object of mind; no realms of elements (from eyes to mind-consciousness); no interdependent origins and no extinction of them (from ignorance to old age and death); no suffering, no origination of suffering, no extinction of suffering, no path; no understanding, no attainment.

"Because there is no attainment, the bodhisattvas, supported by the Perfection of Understanding, find no obstacles for their minds. Having no obstacles, they overcome fear, liberating themselves forever from illusion and realizing perfect Nirvana. All Buddhas in the past, present, and future, thanks to this Perfect Understanding, arrive at full, right, and universal Enlightenment.

"Therefore, one should know that Perfect Understanding is a great mantra, is the highest mantra, is the unequaled mantra, the destroyer of all suffering, the incorruptible truth. A mantra of Prajnaparamita should therefore be proclaimed. This is the mantra:

"*Gate gate paragate parasamgate bodhi svaha.*"

Born in this world
You got to suffer
Everything changes
You got no soul

Try to be gay
Ignorant happy
You get the blues
You eat the jellyroll

There is.one Way
You take the high road
In your big Wheel
8 steps you fly

Look at the View
Right to horizon
Talk to the sky
Act like you talk

Work like the sun
Shine in your heaven
See what you done
Come down & walk

Sit you sit down
Breathe when you breathe
Lie down   you lie down
Walk where you walk

Talk when you talk
Cry when you cry
Lie down   you lie down
Die when you die

Look when you look
Hear what you hear
Taste what you taste   here
Smell what you smell

Touch what you touch
Think what you think
Let go Let it go   Slow
Earth Heaven & Hell

Die when you die
Die when you die
Lie down   you lie down
Die when you die

Allen Ginsberg

Death, Great Death

THE SUSPENSE

Life is dis-
appointing,
So this—or

that's—we say—
what it is?
Death—of course—

is much more
surprising.
But—you'll see.

Cid Corman

Having a body or not having a body—
Is there self or no self—
I ponder deeply like this.
For a long time I sit leaning on the rocks:
green grass comes up around my legs
red dust settles on my head.
Already I see worldly people
offering wine and fruit at my deathbed.

Hanshan

Autumn valley
funeral eve chanting rises
drifts away

Mitsu Suzuki

Dongshan had his head shaved and his body washed, then he put on his robes. He ordered the bell to be rung, and he bid farewell to his community. Then Dongshan sat straight up with dignity, and passed away. The monks wept and could not stop. Dongshan suddenly opened his eyes and said to them, "Those who have left households should not have attachments in their minds. This is true practice. Everyone struggles in life and is upset about death. But what use is it to grieve?"

Then Dongshan asked the monastery director to prepare a feast for offering up delusions. The monks, however, could not cut their attachments, so they stretched out the preparations for seven days.

When the meal was ready, Dongshan joined the monks. At the end of the meal he said, "Monks shouldn't make a big deal about anything. When you see me go this time, don't be agitated."

Then Dongshan went back to the abbot's quarters, sat still, and passed away.

O

This sick pale face doesn't brighten the mirror.
My white hair keeps getting all tangled.
With dry lips, I frequently think of water.
Body so grimy, in vain I wish to be clean.
Cold and heat immediately become noticeable.
Pulse is oddly confused and disordered.
I faintly hear woodcutters talking.
The second month is already half gone.

Ryokan

For many years I dug the ground looking for blue sky,
accumulating layers and layers of mediocrity.
One night in the darkness, the roof tiles were blown
    away.
The bones of emptiness dissolved of themselves.

Muso

ACTUALIZING THE FUNDAMENTAL
POINT

As all things are buddha-dharma, there is delusion and realization, practice, and birth and death, and there are buddhas and sentient beings. As the myriad things are without an abiding self, there is no delusion, no realization, no buddha, no sentient being, no birth and death. The buddha way is, basically, leaping clear of the many and the one; thus there are birth and death, delusion and realization, sentient beings and buddhas. Yet in attachment blossoms fall, and in aversion weeds spread.

To carry yourself forward and experience myriad things is delusion. That myriad things come forth and experience themselves is awakening. Those who have great realization of delusion are buddhas; those who are greatly deluded about realization are sentient beings. Further, there are those who continue realizing beyond realization, who are in delusion throughout delusion. When buddhas are truly buddhas they do not necessarily notice that they are buddhas. However, they are actualized buddhas, who go on actualizing buddhas.

When you see forms or hear sounds fully engaging body-and-mind, you grasp things directly. Unlike things and their reflections in the mirror, and unlike the moon and its reflection in the water, when one side is illuminated the other side is dark.

To study the buddha way is to study the self. To study the self is to forget the self. To forget the self is to be actualized by myriad things. When actualized by myriad things, your body and mind as well as the bodies and minds of others drop away. No trace of realization remains, and this no-trace continues endlessly.

When you first seek dharma, you imagine you are far away from its environs. But dharma is already correctly transmitted; you are immediately your original self.

When you ride in a boat and watch the shore, you might assume that the shore is moving. But when you keep your eyes closely on the boat, you can see that the boat moves. Similarly, if you examine myriad things with a confused body and mind you might suppose that your mind and nature are permanent. When you practice intimately and return to where you are, it will be clear that nothing at all has unchanging self.

Firewood becomes ash, and it does not become firewood again. Yet, do not suppose that the ash is future and the firewood past. You should understand that firewood abides in the phenomenal expression of firewood, which fully includes past and future and is independent of past and future. Ash abides in the phenomenal expression of ash, which fully includes future and past. Just as firewood does not become firewood again after it is ash, you do not return to birth after death. This being so, it is an established way in buddha-dharma to deny that birth turns into death. Accordingly, birth is understood as no-birth. It is an unshakeable teaching in Buddha's discourse that death does not turn into birth. Accordingly, death is understood as no-death. Birth is an expression complete this moment. Death is an expression complete this moment. They are like winter and spring. You do not call winter the beginning of spring, nor summer the end of spring.

Enlightenment is like the moon reflected on the water. The moon does not get wet, nor is the water broken. Although its light is wide and great, the moon is reflected even in a puddle an inch wide. The whole moon and the entire sky are reflected in dewdrops on the grass, or even in one drop of water. Enlightenment does not divide you, just as the moon does not break the water. You cannot hinder enlightenment, just as a drop of water does not hinder the moon in the sky. The depth of the drop is the height of the moon. Each reflection, however long or short its duration, manifests the vastness of the dewdrop, and realizes the limitlessness of the moonlight in the sky.

When dharma does not fill your whole body and mind, you think it is already sufficient. When dharma fills your body and mind, you understand that something is missing. For example, when you sail out in a boat to the middle of an ocean where no land is in sight, and view the four directions, the ocean looks circular, and does not look any other way. But the ocean is neither round nor square; its features are infinite in variety. It is like a palace. It is like a jewel. It only looks circular as far as you can see at that time. All things are like this. Though there are many features in the dusty world and the world beyond conditions, you see and understand only what your eye of practice can reach. In order to learn the nature of the myriad things, you must know that although they may look round or square, the other features of oceans and mountains are infinite in variety; whole worlds are there. It is so not only around you, but also directly beneath your feet, or in a drop of water.

A fish swims in the ocean, and no matter how far it swims there is no end to the water. A bird flies in the sky, and no matter how far it flies there is no end to the air. However, the fish and the bird have never left their elements. When their activity is large their field is large. When their need is small their field is small. Thus, each of them totally covers its full range, and each of them totally experiences its realm. If the bird leaves the air it will die at once. If the fish leaves the water it will die at once.

Know that water is life and air is life. The bird is life and the fish is life. Life must be the bird and life must be the fish. It is possible to illustrate this with more analogies. Practice, enlightenment, and people are like this.

Now if a bird or a fish tries to reach the end of its element before moving in it, this bird or this fish will not find its way or its place. When you find your place where you are, practice occurs, actualizing the fundamental point. When you find your way at this moment, practice occurs, actualizing the fundamental point; for the place, the way, is neither large nor small, neither yours nor others'. The place, the way, has not carried over from the past, and it is not merely arising now. Accordingly, in the practice-enlightenment of the buddha way, meeting one thing is mastering it—doing one practice is practicing completely.

Here is the place; here the way unfolds. The boundary of realization is not distinct, for the realization comes forth simultaneously with the mastery of the buddha-dharma. Do not suppose that what you realize becomes your knowledge and is grasped by your consciousness. Although actualized immediately, the inconceivable may not be apparent. Its appearance is beyond your knowledge.

Zen master Baoche of Mt. Mayu was fanning himself. A monk approached and said, "Master, the nature of wind is permanent and there is no place it does not reach. Why, then, do you fan yourself?"

"Although you understand that the nature of the wind is permanent," Baoche replied, "you do not understand the meaning of its reaching everywhere."

"What is the meaning of its reaching everywhere?" asked the monk again. The master just kept fanning himself. The monk bowed deeply.

The actualization of the buddha-dharma, the vital path of its correct transmission, is like this. If you say that you do not need to fan yourself because the nature of wind is permanent and you can have wind without fanning, you will understand neither permanence nor the nature of wind. The nature of wind is permanent; because of that, the wind of the buddha's house brings forth the gold of the earth and makes fragrant the cream of the long river.

Dogen

Narrow path toward the cemetery
generations of abbots
fallen camellias

Mitsu Suzuki

Birth, old age,
Sickness, and death:
From the beginning,
This is the way
Things have always been.
Any thought
Of release from this life
Will wrap you only more tightly
In its snares.
The sleeping person
Looks for a Buddha,
The troubled person
Turns toward meditation.
But the one who knows
That there's nothing to seek
Knows too that there's nothing to say.
She keeps her mouth closed.

Ngoc Kieu

DEATH POEM

I borrowed this a month ago yesterday.
I return it this month, today.
Out of the five I borrowed I return four,
so I'm clear, except for Original Emptiness.

Ikkyu

My passport should be returned to the Japanese authorities, and the report of my death should be made lawfully. I am a man without a country but, after all, the law is the law. I am a homeless monk, therefore there is nothing to be left to anyone.

Remember me as a monk, and nothing else. I do not belong to any sect or cathedral. None of them should send me a promoted priest's rank or anything of that sort. I like to be free from such trash and die happily.

Nyogen Senzaki

FULL MOON IN THE EIGHTH MONTH
(DEATH POEM)

In autumn
even when I hope
to see it again,
how can I sleep
with the moon this evening?

Dogen

Grandmother's Heart

Beneficial action is skillfully to benefit all classes of sentient beings, that is, to care about their distant and near future, and to help them by using skillful means. In ancient times, someone helped a caged tortoise; another took care of an injured sparrow. They did not expect a reward; they were moved to do so only for the sake of beneficial action.

Foolish people think that if they help others first, their own benefit will be lost; but this is not so. Beneficial action is an act of oneness, benefiting self and others together.

To greet petitioners, a lord of old three times stopped in the middle of his bath and arranged his hair, and three times left his dinner table. He did this solely with the intention of benefiting others. He did not mind instructing even subjects of other lords. Thus you should benefit friend and enemy equally. You should benefit self and others alike. If you have this mind, even beneficial action for the sake of grasses, trees, wind, and water is spontaneous and unremitting. This being so, make a wholehearted effort to help the ignorant.

Dogen

PLEASE CALL ME BY MY TRUE NAMES

Don't say that I will depart tomorrow—
even today I am still arriving.

Look deeply: every second I am arriving
to be a bud on a spring branch,
to be a tiny bird, with still-fragile wings,

learning to sing in my new nest,
to be a caterpillar in the heart of a flower,
to be a jewel hiding itself in a stone.

I still arrive, in order to laugh and to cry,
to fear and to hope.
The rhythm of my heart is the birth and death
of all that is alive.

I am a mayfly metamorphosing
on the surface of the river.
And I am a bird that swoops down to swallow the
    mayfly.

I am a frog swimming happily
in the clear water of a pond.
And I am the grass-snake
that silently feeds itself on the frog.

I am the child in Uganda, all skin and bones,
my legs as thin as bamboo sticks.
And I am the arms merchant,
selling deadly weapons to Uganda.

I am the twelve-year-old girl,
refugee on a small boat,
who throws herself into the ocean
after being raped by a sea pirate.
And I am the pirate,
my heart not yet capable
of seeing and loving.

I am a member of the politburo,
with plenty of power in my hands.
And I am the man who has to pay

his "debt of blood" to my people
dying slowly in a forced-labor camp.

My joy is like Spring, so warm
it makes flowers bloom all over the Earth.
My pain is like a river of tears,
so vast it fills the four oceans.

Please call me by my true names,
so I can hear all my cries and laughter at once,
so I can see that my joy and pain are one.

Please call me by my true names,
so I can wake up
and the door of my heart could be left open,
the door of compassion.

Thich Nhat Hanh

Season's first tea fire
hanging scroll
"Nothing to possess"

Mitsu Suzuki

One life—too lazy to do anything!
I hate heaviness; only light things are convenient.
Other houses study commerce;
I hold a single sutra scroll
with no idea of decorating or mounting it.

Coming and going I save people the carrying.
In response to disease explain medicine.
With skillful means awaken sentient beings.
If only your mind doesn't harbor particulars
what place isn't still and clear?

Hanshan

Layman Pang was sitting in his grass-thatched hut. All of a sudden he said, "Difficult, difficult. It's like trying to cover a tree with ten cups of sesame oil."

His wife heard him and said, "Easy, easy. It's like a hundred grass tips on top of the ancestor's mind."

His daughter said, "Not difficult, not easy. It's like eating rice when hungry, sleeping when tired."

O

When Dongshan was holding a memorial feast for Yunyan, a monk asked, "When you studied with master Yunyan, what kind of instructions did you receive?"

Dongshan said, "Although I studied with him, I didn't receive any instructions."

The monk said, "Since you didn't receive any instructions, why are you offering this feast?"

Dongshan said, "How could I turn away from him?"

The monk continued, "You first studied with Nanquan. So why hold the feast for Yunyan?"

Dongshan said, "It's not that I value Yunyan's virtue, or his buddha-dharma. I just value that he did not try to persuade me."

The monk said, "By holding a feast for your teacher, are you accepting him?"

Dongshan said, "Half accept, and half not."

The monk asked, "Why not accept him entirely?"

Dongshan said, "If I accept him entirely, I'd diminish him."

○

The Fifth Ancestor of Zen in China asked all his disciples to compose a verse showing their understanding. Only the senior monk, Shenxiu, wrote one, and he brushed it onto the wall of the south hall. It read:

> Body is the bodhi tree.
> Mind is a bright mirror on a stand.
> Polish it from time to time;
> don't let it get dusty.

The Fifth Ancestor called all the monks together, burned incense before the verse, and urged them to recite it, saying that if they practiced it they wouldn't fall into evil ways. Privately he remarked to Shenxiu, "This is just arriving at the gate, but not entering," and he asked him to ponder more deeply, and to write another verse.

A young boy recited the verse as he passed by the mill hut, where Huineng was pounding rice. Huineng, who was illiterate, asked the boy, "What kind of verse is that?"

The boy said, "Don't you know? Our master asked each of us to write something expressing our understanding of birth and death. He said that whoever expressed the essential meaning will be given his robe and his dharma. This verse was written by head monk Shenxiu on the wall of the south hall, and the master asked us to recite it."

Huineng said, "I've been pounding rice with this treadle for eight months, and so I haven't been to the Buddha hall yet. Sir, would you please take me to this south hall, so I can see and bow to the verse?"

The boy took him to the south hall and read the verse to him. Huineng understood differently and composed his own verse, which he asked a monk to write for him on another wall. His verse said:

> Bodhi is not a tree.
> Mirror has no stand.
> Buddha nature is always pure;
> how could it get dusty?

The monks saw this verse and became upset, and Huineng went back to the mill hut.

The Fifth Ancestor read the verse and immediately saw that Huineng understood the essential meaning.

At midnight the Fifth Ancestor sent for Huineng and explained the Diamond Sutra to him. On first hearing, Huineng directly understood it. The master said, "I want you to be the Sixth Ancestor," and he gave him his robe as proof. "The robe should be transmitted from generation to generation. Dharma should be transmitted from mind to mind. Each person must realize this themselves."

Fearing that the community would be angry at his having transmitted the dharma to a lowly mill worker, the Fifth Ancestor told Huineng to leave immediately, and not to teach for three years.

○

Once Yunmen said to the assembly: "Medicine and disease cure each other. The entire earth is medicine. What is the self?"

○

HYMNUS AD PATREM SINENSIS

I praise those ancient Chinamen
Who left me a few words,
Usually a pointless joke or a silly question

A line of poetry drunkenly scrawled on the margin
            of a quick splashed picture—bug, leaf,
            caricature of Teacher—
On paper held together now by little more than ink
& their own strength brushed momentarily over it

            Their world and several others since
            Gone to hell in a handbasket, they knew it—
            Cheered as it whizzed by—
& conked out among the busted spring rain cherryblossom
winejars
            Happy to have saved us all

                    Philip Whalen

Explaining a koan to Satsu in a private interview, Hakuin once
said, "Now do you understand?" She responded, "Would you
please explain it again?" Just as he opened his mouth to speak she
interrupted him with, "Thank you for your trouble," and bowed
her way out of the room. Hakuin, looking crestfallen, exclaimed,
"I've been overthrown by this terrible little woman!"

                    O

Students of the Way, when seeing a teacher and learning about dharma, you should listen wholeheartedly, and ask questions repeatedly to have clear understanding. If you do not ask what you should ask or do not say what you should say, it will be your loss.

The teacher usually waits until the student asks, before speaking. Therefore you should ask over and over again, even if you think you understand. The teacher should also ask thoroughly, to make sure the student understands.

Dogen

The beauty of these children is such
that their faces & figures appear to me
to stand out luminous like mountains
more present than what surrounds and continues them
in the constantly conscious
They have been carefully placed here
in violence manifest & in blood & fluid
in front of my eyes which see them daily
in their movements & gestures they wear
as surely as clothes They come animate
facing me & I understand in them
also the meaning of words which move
by their own power, in their own drama
One is always, by the nature of the thing,
made and made to act and act again
in the midst of one's confusion
Here is I think a forward moving thing
& with it much that matters
& some things that do not I

am given this to understand these
children & their voices to caretake
for a time on the earth until
death comes to one of us All love
comes to us for aid in what we cannot
know the way to do, to take the
measure of what we
as the people say "should" do to make
it come out right. Trees let us
always return to trees
for our children's sake to know
how to love them let them grow
as they come & let them then go
a brief moment presently

Norman Fischer

One day Maurine Stuart was having tea with friends at her home in Cambridge when the telephone rang.

"Do Buddhas wear toe-nail polish?" a seven-year-old caller wanted to know.

"Are you wearing toe-nail polish?" Roshi responded.

"YES!" shouted the little girl, and hung up.

Great Doubt

Xingyan said, "Suppose you were high up in a tree, clinging to a branch with just your teeth. Your hands can't reach any branches, and your feet can't touch either. Someone on the ground asks you, 'What is the meaning of Bodhidharma's coming from India?' If you don't speak, you fail the questioner. If you speak, you lose your own life. How do you answer?"

○

Ekaku (Hakuin) gave up sleeping, in his intense effort to break through the barrier of ordinary thinking. Etan blocked him at every turn, rejecting all intellectual interpretations of the koans the student was struggling with. "A pit meditation!" the master shouted whenever Ekaku presented his understanding, suggesting that Ekaku was still trapped in a narrow view.

While this combat was going on, he went one morning to the nearby town of Iiyama for *takuhatsu* or begging—a practice still done by Buddhist monks, who go from door to door carrying a bowl and walking stick with rattling rings on top. Standing at the door of a house and working incessantly on his koans, Ekaku did not notice when a man inside yelled, "Go away, go away!" The man got angry and battered him on the head with a broom handle until Ekaku fell to the ground unconscious. As some passersby helped him to his feet, he opened his eyes and suddenly knew that all the impenetrable koans had been solved. He clapped his hands and burst out laughing. "A crazy monk!" said those who had helped him, and ran away.

Ekaku went back to the monastery, approached Etan, who was standing on the verandah with a fan in his hand, and made a statement which indicated his penetration of the koans. The master responded by stroking Ekaku's back with his fan and saying, "I hope you will live longer than I. You must promise me that you will not be satisfied with minor achievements in whatever you do."

○

Wuzu said, "A water buffalo goes through a louvered window. Head, horns, and all four legs get through. Why can't its tail get through?"

○

Most of the work with a koan takes place alone while sitting zazen, because in reality there's nothing anyone can give us. There's nothing that we lack. Each one of us is perfect and complete, lacking nothing. That's why it is said that there are no Zen teachers and nothing to teach. But this truth must be realized by each one of us. Great faith, great doubt, and great determination are three essentials for that realization. It is a boundless faith in oneself and in the ability to realize oneself and make oneself free, and a deep and penetrating doubt which asks: Who am I? What is life? What is truth? What is God? What is reality? This great faith and great doubt are in dynamic tension with each other, and work to provide the real cutting edge of koan practice. When great faith and great doubt are also accompanied by great determination (the determination of "Seven times knocked down, eight times get up"), we have at our disposal the power necessary to break through our delusive way of thinking and realize the full potential of our lives.

John Daido Loori

The Sixth Ancestor Huineng came across two monks who were arguing about a banner flapping in the wind. One said, "The banner is moving." The other said, "The wind is moving." They went back and forth without coming to agreement.

The Sixth Ancestor said, "It's not that the wind is moving; it's not that the banner moves; it's your mind that is moving." The two monks were stunned.

○

In traditional Zen centers which work with sitting and posture methods, it is often said: "Just sit long enough, and eventually, maybe after many lifetimes, you will come upon the truth." It is also said: "Sitting in the correct posture itself is enlightenment." Is one attached to these ideas?

Maybe one will sit forever and never come upon the truth! Is truth dependent upon sitting? Upon correct posture? Upon anything?

It is dependent on nothing. That's the beauty of it—it depends on nothing. It has no cause, no method, no attainment, no preservation. What is it?

Toni Packer

Once a monk called Director Xuanze was in the assembly of Fayan. Fayan asked him, "Director Xuanze, how long have you been in this community?"

Xuanze said, "I have been studying with you for three years."

The master said, "You are a latecomer. Why don't you ask me about buddha-dharma?"

Xuanze said, "I cannot deceive you, sir. When I was studying with Zen master Qingfeng, I mastered the place of ease and joy in buddha-dharma."

The master said, "With what words did you enter this understanding?"

Xuanze said, "When I asked Qingfeng, 'What is the self of a Zen student?' he said, 'The fire god is here to look for fire.'"

Fayan said, "That is a good statement. But I'm afraid *you* did not understand it."

Xuanze said, "The fire god belongs to fire. So I understood that fire looks for fire and self looks for self."

The master said, "Indeed, you did not understand. If buddha-dharma were like that, it would not have been transmitted until now."

Then Xuanze was distressed and went away. But on his way he said to himself, "The master is a renowned teacher in this country, a great leader of five hundred monks. His criticism of my fault ought to have some point." He went back to Fayan, apologized, and said, "What is the self of a Zen student?"

Fayan said, "The fire god is here to look for fire."

Upon hearing this statement, Xuanze had a great realization of buddha-dharma.

O

Soft spring rain—
since when
have I been called a monk?

Soen Nakagawa

Under the trees, among the rocks, a thatched hut:
verses and sacred commentaries live there together.
I'll burn the books I carry in my bag,
but how can I forget the verses written in my gut?

Ikkyu

Scalding coffee from a freezing cup.
At the rim no telling
Which is which.

Lou Hartman

Emperor Wu of Liang invited layman Fu to expound the Diamond Sutra. Fu took his seat, hit the table once, then got down. Emperor Wu was shocked.

Master Chih asked, "Did you understand that, Your Majesty?"

The emperor said, "Not at all."

Master Chih said, "This layman has completely expounded the sutra."

O

Word will be destroyed by word,
Sword by Sword,
Good by Good.
The sword slashes, slashes the Void
But the sword is broken
And the Void blinks its eyes.

Jung Kwung

NO MATTER, NEVER MIND

The Father is the Void
The Wife   Waves

Their child is Matter.

Matter makes it with his mother
And their child is Life,
                a daughter.

The Daughter is the Great Mother
Who, with her father/brother Matter
                as her lover,

Gives birth to the Mind.

Gary Snyder

SELF-PORTRAIT

Wind-crazy crazy person rouses crazy wind,
comes and goes in whorehouses and sake shops.
Who with the eye of a patch-robe monk will give me a
    try?
Paint South, paint North, paint West, East.

Ikkyu

Aesthetics of Emptiness

When you paint spring, do not paint willows, plums, peaches, or apricots—just paint spring. To paint willows, plums, peaches, or apricots is to paint willows, plums, peaches, or apricots. It is not yet painting spring.

Dogen

ON HIS SELF-PORTRAIT

Loathed by a thousand buddhas in the realm of a
    thousand buddhas,
hated by demons among the troops of demons,
this foul-smelling blind bald-head
appears again on someone's piece of paper.
Damn!

Hakuin

One day a student asked Taiga Ike, "What is the most difficult part of painting?"

Taiga said, "The part of the paper where nothing is painted is the most difficult."

○

Where beauty is, then there is ugliness;
where right is, also there is wrong.
Knowledge and ignorance are interdependent;
delusion and enlightenment condition each other.
Since olden times it has been so.
How could it be otherwise now?
Wanting to get rid of one and grab the other
is merely realizing a scene of stupidity.
Even if you speak of the wonder in it all,
how do you deal with each thing changing?

Ryokan

Not last night,
not this morning;
melon flowers bloomed.

Basho

D. T. Suzuki, when I was studying with him, said the ego has the capacity to cut itself off from experience—whether it comes through the senses or through dreams—and it can also flow with the experience. It has that capacity.

In other words we can change our minds, so that rather than concentrating on our selves in self-consciousness, we can become attentive to environment—outside like today, or it can be, so to speak, zero in the contemplative setting.

I thought that instead of taking the conventional discipline of sitting cross-legged that I would take this other way. If I approach the world of relativity free of my likes and dislikes, so that when something happens that I don't like, instead of continuing to say I don't like it, I ask myself why don't I like it? then here is a clear possibility of changing my mind.

I proceed from one composition to another in a similar way. And then you can take all kinds of things as guides. In other words, you can become an observer of your work and of the effect of your work both on yourself and to a lesser extent on other people.

John Cage

Within this tree
another tree
inhabits the same body;
within this stone
another stone rests,
its many shades of gray
the same, its identical
surface and weight.
And within my body,
another body,
whose history, waiting,
sings: *there is no other body,*
it sings,
there is no other world.

Jane Hirshfield

A room for the way of tea generally faces the north. The reason is that the utensils appear in their real forms when the light is not strong. When the light is bright the utensils look superficial.

Jo'o

A tea spoon should be made in the way that it does not look beautiful.

Rikyu

Those who are nothing particular are noble people. Simply don't strive—just be ordinary.

Linji

The way of tea has nothing to do with discriminating good utensils from bad utensils nor considering the form of making tea. The basic meaning of tea is to realize samadhi while using tea utensils and to practice seeing into the original nature.

Sotan

When mountains and waters are painted, blue, green, and red paints are used, strange rocks and wondrous stones are used, the four jewels and the seven treasures are used.

Rice-cakes are painted in the same manner.

When a person is painted, the four great elements and five skandhas are used.

When a buddha is painted, not only a clay altar or lump of earth is used, but the thirty-two marks, a blade of grass, and the cultivation of wisdom for incalculable eons are used. As a buddha has been painted on a single scroll in this way, all buddhas are painted buddhas, and all painted buddhas are actual buddhas.

Examine a painted buddha, and examine a painted rice-cake. Which is the black stone tortoise, which is the iron staff? Which is form and which is mind? Pursue and investigate this in detail. When you penetrate this matter, the coming and going of birth and death is a painting. Unsurpassed enlightenment is painting. The entire phenomenal universe and the empty sky are nothing but a painting.

Dogen

Who calls my poems poems?
My poems are not poems.
Knowing my poems are not poems,
together we can begin to speak of poems.

Ryokan

A good player of shakuhachi is one who makes the bamboo shaft alive. A master naturally and effortlessly brings forth something inconceivable. However, without study it is impossible to enter the boundaries of mastery.

You become the bamboo. The bamboo becomes you. A master lives in emptiness while working in form. Then playing each piece becomes the ultimate piece "Kyorei (Void Spirit)." Emptiness is taking the name of Kyorei as the essence of each piece.

Emptiness is calling oneself void. The Zen practice of living in emptiness and working in form applies to the self and the heart.

Fuyo Hisamatsu

To have nothing in mind is noble. To have no skill and no knowledge is supreme. No abiding, no hermitage, comes next.

Basho

Kobun Chino Roshi, a Zen master and a master of *kyudo*, the way of the bow, was at Esalen with his archery teacher, who was demonstrating Zen archery. He demonstrated a shot at a target and then he handed the bow and an arrow to Kobun and invited him to demonstrate his skill. Esalen is high on a cliff over the Pacific Ocean, so Kobun took an arrow and the bow and with complete concentration and attention and care, he drew the bow and released the arrow into the ocean! When it hit the water he said, "Bull's eye!"

○

Issan Dorsey was asked, "What is the essence of Zen art?"
He replied, "Nothing extra."

○

An audience sometimes comments that what was not expressed was the most striking part of a performance. This comes from the hidden intention of the actor. Dance, chanting, movement, and gestures are all expressed by the body. What is not expressed is in the gap.

If we consider why this gap can be so striking, the reason is that the actor never relaxes his inner force. In between the dance, chanting, speaking, and gestures, the fullness of the actor's inner force is maintained and this permeates the atmosphere.

Zeami

The Knot

Yesterday by the river I saw trees
too miserably broken to talk about.
Two or three trunks remained
with thousands of ax marks on them.
Frost had stripped off shriveled yellow leaves.
Waves burst on decayed roots.
To love some place is just like this—
what's the use of blaming heaven and earth?

Hanshan

The existence of disability in the human population raises some important questions. What is this Zen work really all about? Is it about sitting in a certain position, in a particular posture, eating soundlessly with chopsticks out of Japanese bowls? I don't think so.

Such a vision excludes a lot of people. My mother, for example. Her hands shake. They always have. She could never eat an oryoki meal without experiencing humiliation and failure.

I'm not opposed to rigorous formal Zen practice . . . but what I am questioning is a certain mentality that actually mistakes these rituals for the truth itself.

Disabled people are a great corrective for a certain strain of Japanese Zen which emphasizes the details of form in such a way that correct technique becomes more important than the heart of the practice. What could be better than having a few visibly imperfect people around who twitch and drool and stumble and make noise and go the wrong way? Imperfection is a beautiful thing. It's the essence of being organic and alive.

Joan Tollifson

In the early 1980s when a movement against the nuclear arms race was surging, a teacher gave a lecture at San Francisco Zen Center and repeated the phrase, "Everything is OK." Someone in the audience asked, "Roshi, do you still say 'Everything is OK' when your country is about to go to war?" Roshi said, "Gee, that's a tough question." The person who asked the question wrote a poem later:

Everything
just as it is,
as it is,
as is.
Flowers in bloom.
Nothing to add.
Nothing to reduce.
The entire world.
Hiroshima.

O

When people talk about war
I vow with all beings
to raise my voice in the chorus
and speak of original peace.

Robert Aitken

SPEL AGAINST DEMONS

The release of Demonic Energies in the name of
                    the People
            must cease

Messing with blood sacrifice in the name of
                    Nature
            must cease

The stifling self-indulgence in anger in the name of
                    Freedom
            must cease

this is death to clarity
death to compassion

the man who has the soul of the wolf
knows the self-restraint
of the wolf

aimless executions and slaughterings
are not the work of wolves and eagles

but the work of hysterical sheep

The Demonic must be devoured!
Self-serving must be
            cut down
Anger must be
            plowed back
Fearlessness, humor, detachment, is power

Gnowledge is the secret of Transformation!

Down with demonic killers who mouth revolutionary
slogans and muddy the flow of change, may they be
Bound by the Noose, and Instructed by the Diamond
Sword of ACHALA the Immovable, Lord of Wisdom,
    Lord
of Heat, who is squint-eyed and whose face is terrible
with bare fangs, who wears on his crown a garland of
severed heads, clad in a tiger skin, he who turns
Wrath to Purified Accomplishment,

whose powers are of lava,
of magma, of deep rock strata, of gunpowder,
                and the Sun.

He who saves tortured intelligent demons and filth-
        eating
                hungry ghosts, his spel is,

NAMAH SAMANTAH VAJRANAM CHANDA
MAHAROSHANA
        SPHATAYA HUM TRAKA HAM MAM

Gary Snyder

Once an envoy from Emperor Dezong came to Lazy Zan's stone hermitage on Mount Heng and said, "Here is an imperial message for you. Stand up and give thanks for his favors, reverend." Lazy Zan brushed aside his cow-dung fire, got a baked taro, and started eating. His nose was dripping and he didn't answer. The messenger laughed and said, "Let me tell you something, reverend, but for the moment wipe off your running nose." Lazy Zan answered, "Why should I trouble to wipe off my nose for a man of the world?"

○

Don't scold or criticize monks with harsh words. Although they make mistakes, don't put them down insensitively. Whatever mistakes they have, if there are more than four monks assembled and practicing together, they should be respected as a treasure of the nation. Abbots, elders, and teachers should give them thorough instruction with a grandmotherly, compassionate mind. Those who should be hit should be hit, and those who should be scolded should be scolded, but don't insult or slander them.

When my late master Rujing was abbot of Tiantong Monastery, he criticized monks and hit them with his slipper during zazen to ward off their dozing. Those who were hit appreciated it, and admired him.

He said in a lecture, "I am old now, and I'm supposed to be retired, and pass my last years in a hut. But I'm here as abbot to help break your delusions, and to assist in your practice of the Way. For this reason, I sometimes scold you, or hit you with a bamboo stick. But this is a dangerous thing to do. I only do this to guide you on behalf of the Buddha. My brothers, please pardon me with compassionate mind." When he said this, all the monks wept.

Dogen

A purple robe—perfect for the "Zen Master."
How can the temple be poor?
Finest silk—worth three hundred strings of green
    copper coins.
Great function appears here.
Fake abbot!
Let me come and see the true thief.

Ikkyu

The aspect of Zen in which I am personally interested is nothing that can be organized, taught, transmitted, certified, or wrapped up in any kind of system. It can't even be followed, for everyone has to find it for himself.

If you do not get it from yourself,
Where will you go for it?

Alan Watts

Thich Nhat Hanh said at Plum Village in France, "There are enough Zen centers. We need more Zen corners."

○

One of the things that is realized when you see the nature of the self is that what you do and what happens to you are the same thing. Realizing that you do not exist separately from everything else, you realize responsibility: you are responsible for everything you experience. You can no longer say, "He made me angry." How could he make you angry? Only you can make you angry. That understanding changes your way of relating to the world and your way of looking at stress. You see that stress is created in your mental processing of your experiences. It usually has to do with separation. Whenever a threat, barrier, or obstacle pops up, our immediate reaction is to pull back, to prepare mentally or physically to fight or run. If you become the barrier—become the fear, the pain, the anger—by experiencing it fully without judging or avoiding or running away, and then let it go, there is no barrier. Actually, there is no way to pull away from it; you cannot run away. There is nowhere to run to, nothing to run from: it is *you*.

John Daido Loori

How pleasant was the body of Chaos:
no rice, also no pissing.
In what encounter were we drilled
so that we have nine holes?
Morning after morning for food and clothes
year after year worry about taxes.
A thousand people fight over one penny,
jostling for their lives, screaming.

Hanshan

FOR WARMTH

I hold my face in my two hands.
No, I am not crying.
I hold my face in my two hands
to keep the loneliness warm—
two hands protecting,
two hands nourishing,
two hands preventing
my soul from leaving me
in anger.

Thich Nhat Hanh

In 1951 at Yale University, Sensei had gone to give a talk on Zen. His audience, consisting of students, professors, and townspeople, was a large and rabid one. After the talk there was a question period, and the first question came from a man with a large shock of white hair and a professorial air. As he rose to ask his question he wrathfully shook his head and brandished his fist.

"Isn't it true," he asked, "that warlords like General Tojo meditated in the Zen monasteries of Japan?"

"Yes." The answer came slowly and softly.

"How compassionate a religion is Zen Buddhism when it allows warlords of his ilk into its temples?"

Dr. Suzuki paused for what seemed like an eternity as the tension mounted among the audience. The silence was thundering. The answer came slowly:

"Don't you think that a soldier, who has to face death many times, needs the solace of religion even more than a civilian?"

Philip Kapleau

A certain Zen teacher celebrated with his students, drinking sake and whiskey until after midnight, then rose next morning before dawn. Peevish, he expressed annoyance that his American students had not risen in time to do zazen before morning service. When they murmured that their sluggishness might be accounted for by all the drink, the teacher snapped, "Sake is one thing, and zazen is another! They have nothing to do with each other!"

O

The more we sit like this, the more we realize the strength of human ignorance. There is no reason why we create this terrible situation, but we do, constantly. . . . This is pretty hard, because the more we taste and chew real peace, the more we realize human ignorance. But the more we realize human ignorance, the more we cannot stop teaching real peace, living real peace.

Dainin Katagiri

There doesn't have to be a need to solve anything, because, as far as I'm concerned, there is no solution. I say that I'm going to end homelessness in ten years, and I believe it. I modify that to say I will end homelessness for those who don't want to be homeless. I don't want to push somebody. I have no doubt (I have to say this very quietly) that there will always be homelessness, but I will work with all my might to eliminate it. If I fail, I fail.

Bernard Tetsugen Glassman

With tropical forests in danger
I vow with all beings
to raise hell with the people responsible
and slash my consumption of trees.

Robert Aitken

WHILE SICK

A precept-breaking monk for eighty yea.s—
still, I'm ashamed of Zen that ignores cause and effect.
Sickness is the result of past karma.
Now how can I honor my endless connections?

Ikkyu

My Teacher once said to me,
   —become one with the knot itself,
   til it dissolves away.
   —sweep the garden.
   — any size.

Gary Snyder

Mountains and Waters

There are mountains hidden in treasures. There are mountains hidden in swamps. There are mountains hidden in the sky. There are mountains hidden in mountains. There are mountains hidden in hiddenness. This is complete understanding.

An ancient buddha said, "Mountains are mountains, waters are waters." These words do not mean mountains are mountains; they mean mountains are mountains.

Therefore investigate mountains thoroughly. When you investigate mountains thoroughly, this is the work of the mountains.

Such mountains and waters of themselves become wise persons and sages.

Dogen

PINE TREE TOPS

in the blue night
frost haze, the sky glows
with the moon
pine tree tops
bend snow-blue, fade
into sky, frost, starlight.
the creak of boots.
rabbit tracks, deer tracks,
what do we know.

Gary Snyder

Sound of Flute
has returned
to bamboo
    Forest

Paul Reps

One day a young monk at Ryutaku-ji had a kensho, and his teacher, seeking to deepen this experience, led him on a long walk up Mount Fuji. Although the monk had seen the great snow mountain many times before, he truly perceived it now for the first time (like the monk who *truly* perceived that the sun was round), and all the way up, he kept exclaiming over the harmony and colors of the wildflowers, the flight of birds, the morning light in the fresh evergreens, the sacred white pine cone! "See how it is made? This stone, it's so . . . so *stone!* Isn't it wonderful? Do you hear the nightingale? It is a miracle! Oh! Fuji-san!"

Muttering a little, the old master hobbled onward, until finally his student noticed his long silence and cried out, "Isn't it so? Aren't these mountains, rivers, and great earth miraculous? Isn't it beautiful?" The old man turned on him. "Yes-s-s," he said forcefully. "But what a pity to *say* so!"

Peter Matthiessen

MESSAGE TO A MONK WHO
SCRIBBLES VERSE

Pain and bliss, love and hate, are like a body and its
    shadow;
Cold and warm, joy and anger, you and your condition.
Delight in singing verse is a road to Hell,
but at Hell's gate—peach blossoms, plum blossoms.

Ikkyu

Spring has hundreds of flowers; autumn, the clear
    moon.
Summer has cool winds; winter has snow.
If busyness doesn't take your mind,
that's your chance.

Wumen

   Man is but a part of the fabric of life—dependent on the
whole fabric for his very existence. As the most highly developed
tool-using animal, he must recognize that the unknown evolu-
tionary destinies of other life forms are to be respected, and act as
gentle steward of the earth's community of being.

Gary Snyder

On the broad river, so vast, the spring day is about to
    dwindle.
Willow blossoms, fluttering about, dot my patched
    robe.
One verse of a fisherman's song inside the dense mist;
this boundless grieving, for whom is it carried on?

Ryokan

It is not only that there is water in the world, but there is a
world in water. It is not just in water. There is also a world of sentient beings in clouds. There is a world of sentient beings in the
air. There is a world of sentient beings in fire. There is a world of
sentient beings on earth. There is a world of sentient beings in
the phenomenal world. There is a world of sentient beings in a
blade of grass. There is a world of sentient beings in one staff.

Wherever there is a world of sentient beings, there is a world
of buddha ancestors. You should thoroughly examine the meaning of this.

Dogen

Daowu visited the assembly of Shitou and asked, "What is the fundamental meaning of buddha-dharma?"

Shitou said, "Not to attain, not to know."

Daowu said, "Is there some turning point in going beyond, or not?"

Shitou said, "The vast sky does not hinder white clouds from flying."

O

Without desire everything is sufficient.
With seeking myriad things are impoverished.
Plain vegetables can soothe hunger.
A patched robe is enough to cover this bent old body.
Alone I hike with a deer.
Cheerfully I sing with village children.
The stream under the cliff cleanses my ears.
The pine on the mountain top fits my heart.

Ryokan

ROSHI

Roshi poured me a glass of Courvoisier. We were in a
   cabin on Mt. Baldy, summer of 1977. We were
   listening to the crickets.
—Kone, Roshi said, you should write a cricket poem.
—I've already written a cricket poem. It was in this
   cabin two years ago.
—Oh

Roshi fried some sliced pork in sunflower oil and boiled
   a three-minute noodle soup. We finished one bottle
   of Courvoisier and opened another.
—Yah, Kone, you should write cricket poem.
—That is a very Japanese idea, Roshi.
—So.

We listened to the crickets a while longer. Then we
   closed the light so we could open the door and get
   the breeze without the flies coming in.
—Yah, Cricket.
—Roshi, give me your idea of a cricket poem.
—Ha ha. Okay:
dark night (said Roshi)
cricket sound break out
cricket girlfriend listening.
—That's pretty good, Roshi.
Dark night (Roshi began again)
walking on the path
suddenly break out cricket sound
where is my lover?
—I don't like that one.
cricket! cricket! (Roshi cried)
you are my lover

now I am walking path by alone
but I am not lonely with you.
—I'm afraid not, Roshi. The first one was good.
Then the crickets stopped for a while and Roshi poured
    the Courvoisier into our glasses. It was a peaceful
    night.
—Yah, Kone, said Roshi very softly. You should write
    more sad.

Leonard Cohen

Sound of mountain
sound of ocean
everywhere spring rain

Soen Nakagawa

Circle

Shunryu Suzuki was gravely sick in bed in San Francisco. A student came to him and said, "Roshi, where shall we meet?" Suzuki Roshi's two hands came out from under the cover with palms together, and made a gassho. Then holding one hand still, he drew a clockwise circle in the air with his other hand. He put his palms back together and made another gassho.

O

The great road has no gate.
It leaps out from the heads of all of you.
The sky has no road.
It enters into my nostrils.
In this way we meet as Gautama's bandits,
or Linji's troublemakers. Ha!
Great houses tumble down and spring wind swirls.
Astonished, apricot blossoms fly and scatter—red.

Rujing

Go sit on the sixteenth-night koan.
When body's moon tries for fullness,
mind moon starts to fade.
If you have a clear idea of moon, a moon will be born.
But how can mid-autumn moon be grasped?

Dogen

The refreshing air wells up
from the bottom of my breath
and pours over my head.
What a pleasant evening.

Shunpo Blanche Hartman

We go into the darkness, we seek initiation, in order to know directly how the roots of all beings are tied together: how we are related to all things, how this relationship expresses itself in terms of interdependence, and finally how all phenomena abide within one another. Yes, the roots of all living things are tied together. Deep in the ground of being, they tangle and embrace. This understanding is expressed in the term *nonduality*. If we look deeply, we find that we do not have a separate self-identity, a self that does not include sun and wind, earth and water, creatures and plants, and one another. We cannot exist without the presence and support of the interconnecting circles of creation—the geosphere, the biosphere, the hydrosphere, the atmosphere, and the sphere of our sun. All are related to us; we depend on each of these spheres for our very existence.

Joan Halifax

Ed Brown: What power will you use to direct others?

Sojun: One time, in dokusan, I asked Suzuki Roshi, "What is power?" He said, "Don't use it."

Ed: What will you use to direct others?

Sojun: You turn me, and I'll turn you.

○

Nanquan, Guizong, and Mayu were on their way to see Master Nanyang. Halfway there, Nanquan drew a circle on the ground and said, "If you understand it, we'll go."

Guizong sat in the middle of the circle. Mayu made a curtsy. Nanquan said, "If this is so, we don't need to go."

Guizong said, "What makes you think so?"

○

A monk asked Quianfeng, "It is said, 'World-Honored Ones in the ten directions are on one path to nirvana.' Where would that path be?"

Quianfeng picked up his stick, drew a line, and said, "Here it is."

CIRCULAR PORTRAIT: IKKYU AND MORI

The monk's entire body is present in this great circle.
Xutang's true face and eye emerge from it.
The blind singer's love song delights
flowers for ten thousand springs.

Ikkyu

ON OPENING THE RING OF BONE
ZENDO

Oh, all you women who chewed hides,
you men who chipped flint,
you squirrels and deer and flickers
    who have bred here and gone and come again,
you pines and oaks and springs and boulders,
we are your children—
we place ourselves in your mountains;
lend us your power
that we may empower the earth
in our turn.

Oh, all you healers of the human heart,
you Buddhas coming forth as words of perfect wisdom,
you Bodhisattvas and guardians of the vast
    and fathomless Dharma,

you teachers of the Three Cloud Halls,
we are your children—
we place ourselves in your realm of great compassion;
lend us your power
that we may fully realize your vows
in our turn.

Robert Aitken

Search

Vigorously cutting a path through the brambles, you
   look for the ox;
rivers wide, mountains far, the path gets longer.
Running out of strength, mind exhausted, you cannot
   find it.
Rustling of maple leaves,
singing of evening cicadas.

Finding traces

By the water, deep within the forest, you find traces.
Leaving fragrant grasses behind, you study the signs.
Following the tracks, you enter endless mountains.
Distant sky—how can the tip of its nose be hidden
   elsewhere?

Seeing

Chirping, a yellow oriole on a branch.
Warm sun, gentle breeze, green willows on the bank.
No place to turn around—
in brambles, its head and horn are not clearly seen.

Catching

Through tremendous effort you have caught the ox.
Still its will is strong, its body vigorous.
Sometimes it runs to a high ground
sometimes it disappears deep in mist.

Taming

You cannot put whip and tether aside
for fear it will wander into a swamp.
Once trained to be gentle
free of rope the ox follows your way.

Riding home

Taking a winding path you ride the ox home.
The tune of your rustic flute permeates the evening
   haze.
Each note, each song: feeling unbounded
knowing the sound is beyond lips and mouth.

Forgetting it

You have ridden home on the ox.
At rest, you forget it.
Bright sun high in the sky, you daydream blissfully
leaving whip and tether behind in the grass-roof hut.

Forgetting all

Whip and tether, you, the ox all empty.
Vast blue sky cannot be reached by ideas.
How can the fire's flame sustain the snowflakes?
Having reached here, you are in accord with the ancient
   way.

Returning to the source

You have returned to the source; effort is over.
The intimate self is blind and deaf.
Inside the hut, nothing outside is seen.
Waters are boundless, flowers red.

Entering the marketplace with giving hands

You go into the marketplace barefooted, unadorned,
smeared with mud, covered with dust, smiling.
Using no supernatural power
you bring the withered trees to bloom.

Kuoan

On the great road of buddha ancestors there is always unsurpassable continuous practice. It forms the way-ring and is never cut off. Throughout aspiration for enlightenment, practice, enlightenment, and nirvana, there is no gap; continuous practice is the circle of the way. This being so, continuous practice is unstained, not forced by you or others. The act of this continuous practice confirms you as well as others. That means your practice affects the entire earth and sky in ten directions. Although it is not noticed by others or by yourself, it is so. In this way, by the continuous practice of all buddhas and ancestors, your practice is actualized and your great road opens up. By your continuous practice, the continuous practice of all buddhas is actualized and the great road of all buddhas opens up. Your continuous practice creates the circle of the way.

Dogen

Notes

People ask for the road to Cold Mountain . . . (p. 2)

Hanshan was a legendary Chinese poet of the late eighth and early ninth centuries. *Han shan* means "cold mountain." This is his name, his dwelling place, and his experience of austere nonduality. His poems were studied widely by Chinese and Japanese monks. Hanshan and his friend Shide have also been favorite subjects for the Zen painters; portrayed as somewhat disheveled and laughing together, Hanshan is usually shown holding a scroll, while Shide carries a broom. Translated by the editors.

Which way . . . (p. 2)

A *waka*—a thirty-one-syllable Japanese poem—by Soto School monk Daigu Ryokan (1658–1731). Ryokan lived alone in a mountain hut, and practiced begging in the villages near the Sea of Japan. During his life he was known for his love of playing with the village children for hours on end. After his death, he was recognized as one of Japan's greatest poets and calligraphers. Translated by Daniel Leighton and Kazuaki Tanahashi.

It was the year 1953 . . . (p. 3)

Philip Kapleau Roshi founded Rochester Zen Center and became one of the first American Zen teachers. His first book, *The Three Pillars of Zen,* provided an introduction to Zen for many of the current generation of practitioners. This section is reprinted with permission from *The Soen Roku: The Sayings and Doings of Master Soen* (New York: Zen Studies Society Press, 1986).

He was offered the whole world . . . (p. 5)

Jung Kwung is a Korean monk and painter. Reprinted with permission from *The Dirty Mop: Unlimited Action Paintings and Poems by Jung Kwung, the Mad Monk,* text by Lewis R. Lancaster, poems translated by Paik Seung-Gil (Berkeley, CA: Asian Humanities Press, 1983).

Ox (p. 5)

Ikkyu Sojun (1394–1481), a monk of the Rinzai School, was born an illegitimate son of Emperor Gokomatsu, and studied Zen with Kaso Sodon, a strict disciplinarian. Known both as a serious practitioner and as an outrageous iconoclast, Ikkyu made no secret of his love for wine, women, and meat, and he called himself Kyounshi ("Crazy Wind Person"). Eventually he became abbot of Daitoku-ji in Kyoto, Rinzai Zen's most prestigious training monastery of that time. His poems are considered among Zen's finest. Translated by the editors.

Awakened within a dream . . . (p. 5)

An English haiku titled "L'Envoi." Lou Hartman is a monk at San Francisco Zen Center, where he has practiced for several decades.

Once seventeen monks from Szechwan were traveling . . . (p. 6)

Yangshan Huiji (803–887) was a famous Chinese teacher of his day. Opposed by his parents, he cut off two fingers to show his determination to become a monk. This story the monks are discussing—about the Sixth Ancestor, Dajian Huineng of China (638–713)—is presented in full in the "Great Doubt" chapter of this book. Translated by the editors.

Some old papers were recently excavated . . . (p. 6)

Nyogen Senzaki (1876–1958), of the Rinzai School, was the first Japanese Zen teacher who taught in the United States as resident, supporting himself with a number of menial jobs. During World War II he was placed in a relocation camp, where he continued to teach Zen.

Bodhidharma, a legendary teacher who brought Zen teaching from India to China, was traditionally called the monk with blue eyes. He is known as the First Ancestor of Zen in China, and his portrait is the most popular motif with Zen painters. He is usually shown with a fierce expression and bulging eyes.

Translated from Japanese by Eido Shimano Roshi. Reprinted with permission from *Like a Dream, Like a Fantasy: The Zen Writings and Translations of Nyogen Senzaki,* edited by Eido Shimano (Tokyo: Japan Publications, 1978).

Rags and again rags . . . (p. 7)

Translated by Daniel Leighton and Kazuaki Tanahashi.

In winter . . . (p. 7)

Soen Nakagawa (1907–1984), of the Rinzai School, was abbot of Ryu-taku-ji Monastery in Japan. He taught in the United States with Nyogen Senzaki, and later with Eido Shimano Roshi. He is regarded as one of the finest Zen haiku poets of this century. Translated by Sherry Chayat and Kazuaki Tanahashi.

We're here to get our present model repainted . . . (p. 8)

Charlotte Joko Beck is the author of two books, *Everyday Zen* and *Nothing Special.* She teaches at the Zen Center in San Diego. Excerpt from *Nothing Special: Living Zen* by Charlotte Joko Beck. Copyright © 1993 by Charlotte Joko Beck. Reprinted by permission of HarperCollins Publishers, Inc.

From now on . . . (p. 8)

Basho Matsuo (1644–1694) was a lay Zen practitioner and the creator of haiku poetry. His works are fundamental classics of Japanese literature. Translated by the editors.

SKILLFUL GUIDANCE

A monk challenged Zhaozhou, "I've been hearing . . ." (p. 10)

Zhaozhou Congshen (778–897), an early Chinese master, was one of the most brilliant teachers in all of Zen history. He began practicing when he was sixty years old, taught for forty years at Guanyin Monastery, and lived to the age of one hundred twenty. His interactions with other monks became the subject of many of the koans.

In this story the monk seems to be asking about a physical aspect of the area, but is instead challenging the master himself. This wordplay is possible because Zen teachers were often known by the names of the mountain or county in which they resided. "Zhaozhou" means "Zhao County."

Quoted from *Blue Cliff Record,* compiled in China by Yuanwu Kequin in 1300; case 52. Translated by the editors.

As a young Zen student, Richard Baker . . . (p. 10)

Richard Baker Roshi teaches at Crestone Mountain Zen Center in Colorado, and at the numerous locations of Dharmasangha, the organizational name for his students in America and Europe. His book *Original Mind: The Practice of Zen in the West* is forthcoming in 1995 from Riverhead/Putnam.

Nanquan was on the mountain working . . . (p. 10)

Nanquan Puyan (748–834) lived simply at Mount Nanquan, as abbot of the monastery there. He spent his days in meditation and farm labor.

This story is found in the Chinese text *Five Lamps Merged in the Source.* Translated by Arnold Kotler and Kazuaki Tanahashi. Reprinted with permission from *Moon in a Dewdrop,* edited by Kazuaki Tanahashi (San Francisco: North Point Press, 1985; currently distributed by Farrar Straus Giroux, New York, and Element Books, Shaftesbury, Dorset, England).

When samadhi develops . . . (p. 11)

Samadhi is a Sanskrit word meaning concentration with or without an object—a collected, settled state of mind. John Daido Loori is the abbot of Zen Mountain Monastery in Mt. Tremper, New York. Reprinted with permission from *Mountain Record of Zen Talks,* by John Daido Loori (Boston: Shambhala Publications, 1988).

Dongshan once taught the assembly . . . (p. 11)

Dongshan Liangjie (807–869) was an influential early Chinese master. He entered the monastery as a child, and studied with several famous teachers. He is considered a cofounder of the Caodong School, and his poem "Song of the Bright Mirror Samadhi" became an important text for Zen students, and remains so to the present day; it is presented in the "Daily Reminders" chapter of this book.

This story was quoted by Eihei Dogen in "Going Beyond Buddha," in *Treasury of the True Dharma Eye.* Translated by Sojun Mel Weitsman and Kazuaki Tanahashi. Reprinted with permission from *Moon in a Dewdrop,* edited by Kazuaki Tanahashi (San Francisco: North Point Press, 1985).

A monk asked, "What is the mind . . . " (p. 12)

Nanyang Huizhong (d. 775) taught Zen for forty years in Nanyang, China. He was considered a great master of the Northern School of Zen, and he emphasized scriptural studies. Because Emperor Suzong asked him to be his teacher, he was known as National Teacher Nanyang. This story is found in *Recorded Sayings of Dongshan.* Translated by the editors.

Zen mind is not Zen mind . . . (p. 12)

Master Sueng Sahn, from Korea, is the founder of Providence Zen Center, in Providence, Rhode Island. Reprinted with permission from *Only Don't Know: The Teaching Letters of Zen Master Sueng Sahn* (Cumberland: Primary Point Foundation, 1985). © 1982 Providence Zen Center.

Layman Pang was sitting casually reading a sutra . . . (p. 13)

This story refers to Pangyan (d. 808), who lived at the time of the earliest Chinese teachers and was a student of Mazu Daoyi. He met many great teachers, and his interactions with them were incorporated into several of the koans. He supported the family by making baskets, which his daughter sold. This story is found in *Recorded Sayings of Layman Pang.* Translated by the editors.

During an early sesshin with Suzuki Roshi . . . (p. 13)

Shunryu Suzuki Roshi (1904–1971), from Japan, founded San Francisco Zen Center and Tassajara Zen Mountain Center, the first training monastery in America. His book of talks, *Zen Mind, Beginner's Mind,* is one of the most widely read books of Zen teachings in the Western world.

A *sesshin* is a concentrated retreat time (usually a week) of Zen meditation. *Dokusan* is a private interview between teacher and student. A *zendo* is a meditation hall in the Zen tradition.

Tenshin Reb Anderson teaches at San Francisco Zen Center.

Zhaozhou went to a hermitage . . . (p. 14)

Quoted from *Gateless Barrier,* case 11. Translated by the editors.

Seung Sahn would say . . . (p. 15)

This story was collected in the 1980s.

There were several monks in residence with Hakuin . . . (p. 15)

Hakuin Ekaku (1685–1768) restored the koan tradition in Japanese Rinzai Zen. Although he lived in a small country temple, his disciples spread his teaching widely, and all present-day Rinzai Zen practitioners are his dharma descendants. Hakuin posed the famous question "What is the sound of one hand clapping?" His painting and calligraphy are extremely powerful and often rough, but are regarded as unsurpassed in Japanese Zen. Reprinted with permission from *Penetrating Laughter: Hakuin's Zen and Art,* by Kazuaki Tanahashi (Woodstock, NY: Overlook Press, 1984).

On the fourth day of sesshin . . . (p. 16)

Ed Brown lives in Marin County, California, and teaches at San Francisco Zen Center. He worked as a cook at Green Gulch Farm, Tassajara, and other Buddhist centers. He began Zen practice under Shunryu Suzuki

Roshi. His publications include the world-famous *Tassajara Bread Book*, and *Tassajara Cooking*. This story is adapted from one told by Ed Brown in "Reminiscences of Suzuki Roshi," *Wind Bell*, fall 1986.

A monk asked Dongshan, "When cold or heat comes . . ." (p. 16)

This story is taken from Eihei Dogen's "Everyday Activity," in *Treasury of the True Dharma Eye*. Translated by Katherine Thanas and Kazuaki Tanahashi. Reprinted with permission from *Moon in a Dewdrop*, edited by Kazuaki Tanahashi (San Francisco: North Point Press, 1985).

When Nyogen was dismissed from his job . . . (p. 17)

Reprinted with permission from *Like a Dream, Like a Fantasy: The Zen Writings and Translations of Nyogen Senzaki*, edited by Eido Shimano (Tokyo: Japan Publications, 1978). Soyen Shaku (1859–1919) was the abbot of the Rinzai monastery Engakù-ji in Kamakura. He came to the United States in 1893 to attend the World Parliament of Religions. There, he made the first formal presentation of Zen Buddhism in America. Soyen Shaku was also the teacher of the famous writer-translator D. T. Suzuki.

A student asked Soen Nakagawa . . . (p. 17)

Reprinted with permission from *33 Fingers: A Collection of Modern American Koans*, by Michael Wenger (San Francisco: Clear Glass Press, 1994).

JUST SITTING

When I was in China in a Zen monastery . . . (p. 20)

Eihei Dogen (1200–1253), one of the foremost figures of Japanese philosophy and letters, was among the first Japanese monks to travel to China and transmit Zen back to Japan. His main work, *Treasury of the True Dharma Eye*, is an extensive collection of essays based on his oral teachings. He is the founder of the Soto School in Japan. The story is quoted from *Treasury of the True Dharma Eye: Record of Things Heard*, a collection of Dogen's informal talks compiled by Koun Ejo. Translated by the editors.

Zhaozhou asked Nanquan . . . (p. 21)

Quoted from *Gateless Barrier*, case 19. Translated by the editors.

On Zazen Practice (p. 21)

A *waka* by Eihei Dogen. Translated by Brian Unger and Kazuaki Tanahashi. Reprinted with permission from *Moon in a Dewdrop,* edited by Kazuaki Tanahashi (San Francisco: North Point Press, 1985).

If there is no clear awareness . . . (p. 22)

Toni Packer is the founder of the Springwater Center for Meditation Inquiry and Retreats in Springwater, New York. Reprinted with permission from her book *The Work of This Moment* (Springwater, NY: Springwater Center, 1988).

Now, all ancestors and all buddhas . . . (p. 22)

From Dogen's "On the Endeavor of the Way," in *Treasury of the True Dharma Eye.* Translated by Ed Brown and Kazuaki Tanahashi. Reprinted with permission from *Moon in a Dewdrop,* edited by Kazuaki Tanahashi (San Francisco: North Point Press, 1985).

At dawn sitting, I imagine . . . (p. 23)

Peter Matthiessen is a Zen teacher and writer who lives in Sagaponack, New York. Among his many books is the award-winning *The Snow Leopard.* Reprinted with permission from *Nine-Headed Dragon River: Zen Journals, 1969–1985,* by Peter Matthiessen (Boston: Shambhala Publications, 1985).

Be soft in your practice . . . (p. 23)

Master Sheng-yen teaches at Ch'an Meditation Center in Elmhurst, New York. Reprinted with permission from "Words of Encouragement," *Ch'an Magazine,* winter 1992.

The notion that the koan . . . (p. 23)

Robert Aitken Roshi founded and teaches at Diamond Sangha in Honolulu, Hawaii. Reprinted with permission from "Words from Roshi," *Diamond Sangha Newsletter,* February 1993.

For half a year just having rice . . . (p. 24)

Tiantong Rujing (1163–1228), a Caodong School monk, was Dogen's teacher in China. Rujing was sixty-two years old and the abbot of the monastery at Tiantong in China when he met the young Japanese monk Dogen in 1225. Recognizing Dogen's potential, Rujing gave him permission to come to his quarters for instruction at any time of day or night, whether in formal or informal robe.

Rujing eschewed the fancy brocade robes he had inherited, and he forbade his students any close contact with kings or ministers. He ignored sectarian differences between the Zen schools of the day, and even denied that Zen itself constituted a special transmission of Buddhism.

An ardent meditator into his old age, he personally led his monks in late-night practice sessions, and was up again early for the morning sittings. Rujing taught his disciples to dispense with chanting, reciting Buddha's name, and any other rituals, and to practice only the pure, single-minded sitting that came to be called *shikan taza* in Japan.

This poem was quoted in Dogen's "Everyday Activity," in *Treasury of the True Dharma Eye*. Translated by Katherine Thanas and Kazuaki Tanahashi. Reprinted with permission from *Moon in a Dewdrop*, edited by Kazuaki Tanahashi (San Francisco: North Point Press, 1985).

A gentle rain settles the dust . . . (p. 24)

This poem is from statements Ed Brown made at the conclusion of a sesshin. Reprinted with permission from *Wind Bell*, winter 1983.

In this world of dreams . . . (p. 25)

A *waka* by Daigu Ryokan. Translated by Daniel Leighton and Kazuaki Tanahashi.

If you're afraid of being grabbed by God . . . (p. 25)

Jiyu Kennett Roshi teaches at Shasta Abbey in Mt. Shasta, California. Her publications include *How to Grow a Lotus Blossom*. Reprinted with permission from *Meeting with Remarkable Women: Buddhist Teachers in America*, by Lenore Friedman (Boston: Shambhala Publications, 1987).

Meditating deeply upon dharma . . . (p. 25)

A Chinese-style poem translated from Japanese by Eido Shimano Roshi. Reprinted with permission from *Like a Dream, Like a Fantasy: The Zen Writings and Translations of Nyogen Senzaki*, edited by Eido Shimano (Tokyo: Japan Publications, 1978).

Now I would like to talk about our zazen posture . . . (p. 26)

From *Zen Mind, Beginner's Mind*, by Shunryu Suzuki (New York and Tokyo: Weatherhill, 1970).

Inside the zendo also . . . (p. 30)

Translated by Sherry Chayat and Kazuaki Tanahashi.

CHOPPING WOOD

It is hard . . . (p. 32)

Gary Snyder was first thrust into the public light as Japhy Ryder, the fictional hero of Jack Kerouac's *The Dharma Bums*. Beginning in 1956, Snyder spent several years studying Zen in Japan, first with Isshu Miura Roshi, and then with Sesso Oda Roshi. He is the author of many books of poetry and essays, including the Pulitzer Prize–winning *Turtle Island*. Gary Snyder, *Turtle Island*, © 1974 by Gary Snyder. Reprinted by permission of New Directions Publishing Corporation.

While thinking about the future . . . (p. 32)

Quoted from *Treasury of the True Dharma Eye: Record of Things Heard*, compiled by Koun Ejo. Translated by the editors.

A woman was pouring tea for guests . . . (p. 33)

Thich Nhat Hanh, a Vietnamese monk, poet, and peace activist, teaches in Plum Village in southern France. He was chair of the Buddhist Peace Delegation to the Paris Peace Accords during the Vietnam War. He was nominated for the Nobel Peace Prize by Martin Luther King Jr. Among his many books of talks and translations is the best-selling *Peace Is Every Step*. This story was collected in 1990.

Either hoeing the garden . . . (p. 33)

Peter Levitt is a poet who lives in Santa Monica, California, and practices Zen at Sonoma Mountain Zen Center. Reprinted with permission from *One Hundred Butterflies*, by Peter Levitt (Seattle: Broken Moon Press, 1992).

Our goals in this practice of nonattainment . . . (p. 34)

Katherine Thanas teaches at Santa Cruz and Monterey Bay Zen Centers. Reprinted with permission from *Sangha Newsletter of Santa Cruz and Monterey Bay Zen Centers*, winter 1994.

Zen monastery . . . (p. 34)

A haiku and comments, by Soen Nakagawa. Translated by Sherry Chayat and Kazuaki Tanahashi.

For a Zen student . . . (p. 35)

Sojun Mel Weitsman teaches at Berkeley Zen Center and San Francisco Zen Center. Reprinted with permission from "Lecture, June 16, 1988," *Wind Bell*, spring 1989.

What a laugh! . . . (p. 35)

An English haiku, titled "First Sesshin with Suzuki Roshi" by Lou Hartman.

Song of the Grass-Roof Hermitage (p. 36)

Shitou Xiqian (700–790) was an early Chinese Zen master. He was called one of Zen's two "great jewels" (the other was Mazu Daoyi). For some years, he meditated continually in a hut built on a rock at Nan Monastery, and was thus called Shitou ("Priest Rock Head"). Translated by Daniel Leighton and Kazuaki Tanahashi. Reprinted with permission from *Cultivating the Empty Field: The Silent Illumination of Zen Master Hongzhi*, by Daniel Leighton (San Francisco: North Point Press, 1991).

In this assembly . . . (p. 37)

Bankei Yotaku (1633–1693) was a Rinzai monk in Edo-period Japan. After a severe fourteen-year quest, he attained his first enlightenment just as he was teetering near death with tuberculosis. Having recovered his health, he continued his practice. A teacher for forty-five years, he stressed the concept of "Unborn" Zen, which emphasized original, inherent enlightenment. Translated by the editors.

If you saw . . . (p. 38)

From *Thank You and OK: An American Zen Failure in Japan*, by David Chadwick (New York: Penguin, 1994).

Americans like to refer to . . . (p. 39)

Reprinted with permission from *Mountain Record of Zen Talks*, by John Daido Loori (Boston: Shambhala Publications, 1988).

Lilacs—peeling stucco—vines . . . (p. 40)

Miriam Sagan is a poet who lives in Santa Fe, New Mexico. Her publications include *True Body* (Berkeley: Parallax Press, 1991).

A moment's absence . . . (p. 40)

Yantou Quanhuo (828–882) was a dharma heir of Deshan Xuanjian in China. Ironically, Yantou was killed by a bandit; he gave a great shout, then died with perfect composure. These words and Yantou's story perplexed the young Hakuin. Later Hakuin quoted them often, and used them as an artistic theme. Reprinted with permission from *Penetrating Laughter: Hakuin's Zen and Art,* by Kazuaki Tanahashi (Woodstock, NY: Overlook Press, 1982).

CLOUD WATER ASSEMBLY

One of the Chinese names for a monk is "cloud-water." The implication is that monks should be free; they should float like a cloud and reflect like water.

Monastery gate . . . (p. 42)

Mitsu Suzuki, wife of Shunryu Suzuki Roshi, is a haiku poet. She taught tea ceremony at San Francisco Zen Center and currently lives in Shizuoka, Japan. Reprinted with permission from *Temple Dusk: Zen Haiku,* by Mitsu Suzuki, translated by Kazuaki Tanahashi and Gregory Wood (Berkeley: Parallax Press, 1992).

When serving a welcoming tea . . . (p. 42)

From *Guidelines for Monastery Officers.* Translated by Sojun Mel Weitsman and Kazuaki Tanahashi.

Temple Rules (p. 43)

"On Keeping the Bodhi Mind" is the first of seven temple rules. Reprinted with permission from *Only Don't Know: The Teaching Letters of Zen Master Seung Sahn* (Cumberland: Primary Point Foundation, 1985). © 1982 Providence Zen Center.

A Thousand Prostrations (p. 44)

Allen Hoey is a poet living in King of Prussia, Pennsylvania. He practices at the Zen Center of Syracuse.

The essence of the Monastery Director's work . . . (p. 44)

From *Guidelines for Monastery Officers.* Translated by Sojun Mel Weitsman and Kazuaki Tanahashi.

I had only been given the opportunity . . . (p. 45)

A *gassho* is a bow made with palms together.

Dusk surrounds the canyon . . . (p. 47)

Reprinted with permission from *Temple Dusk: Zen Haiku*, by Mitsu Suzuki, translated by Kazuaki Tanahashi and Gregory Wood (Berkeley: Parallax Press, 1992).

Sayings of a Zen Master (p. 47)

Kyong Ho (1849–1912) was the great-grand-teacher of Master Sueng Sahn. From *Thousand Peaks: Korean Zen—Traditions and Teachers*, by Mu Soeng Sunim (Berkeley: Parallax Press, 1987).

Yaoshan was an ancient buddha . . . (p. 49)

Yaoshan Weiyan (745–828) was a Chinese master famous for expressing the buddha-dharma in terse single phrases. Quoted from Dogen's *Guidelines for Monastery Officers*. Translated by Sojun Mel Weitsman and Kazuaki Tanahashi.

Dongshan asked a monk . . . (p. 49)

From *Recorded Sayings of Dongshan*. Translated by the editors.

"Harada talked a lot about listening . . ." (p. 49)

A *teisho* is a formal Zen talk. Sogaku Harada Roshi (1871–1961), abbot of Hosshin-ji in Obama, Japan, was an influential teacher for American Zen. Several early Zen teachers in America, including Taizan Maezumi Roshi, founder of the Zen Center of Los Angeles, and Philip Kapleau Roshi, founder of Rochester Zen Center, had a chance to study directly with him, and with his disciple Hakuun Yasutani Roshi (1885–1973). Bernard Tetsugen Glassman teaches at the Zen Community of New York in Yonkers, where social and community service is an integral part of the practice. Reprinted with permission from *Nine-Headed Dragon River: Zen Journals, 1969–1985*, by Peter Matthiessen (Boston: Shambhala Publications, 1985).

Shakyamuni's Austerities (p. 50)

Translated by the editors.

December (p. 50)

Gary Snyder, *The Back Country*, © 1968 by Gary Snyder. Reprinted by permission of New Directions Publishing Corporation.

As you like Zen Center so much . . . (p. 52)

From a lecture by Shunryu Suzuki Roshi at Zen Mountain Center in Tassajara, California, on July 26, 1971. Reprinted with permission from *Wind Bell,* spring 1983.

HOW TO COOK ENLIGHTENMENT

Dongshan asked Yunju, "What are you doing . . ." (p. 54)

From *Recorded Sayings of Dongshan.* In this dialogue, Yunju is the disciple, Dongshan his teacher. Translated by the editors.

An ancient master said, "When you boil rice . . ." (p. 54)

From Dogen's "Instruction for the Tenzo." Translated by Arnold Kotler and Kazuaki Tanahashi. Reprinted with permission from *Moon in a Dewdrop,* edited by Kazuaki Tanahashi (San Francisco: North Point Press, 1985).

Farmers rest in the hot month . . . (p. 54)

In the Indian Buddhist cosmology, Mount Sumeru is at the center of concentric rings of huge mountains; the implication is that it is at the center of the universe. Translated from Chinese by the editors.

Xuefeng was once tenzo . . . (p. 55)

Xuefeng Yican (822–908). Another possible way of translating this story is that Xuefeng overturns the rice-washing bowl. From Dogen's "Instruction for the Tenzo." Translated by Arnold Kotler and Kazuaki Tanahashi. From *Moon in a Dewdrop,* edited by Kazuaki Tanahashi (San Francisco: North Point Press, 1985).

Watermelons and Zen students . . . (p. 55)

Reprinted with permission from *One Hundred Butterflies,* by Peter Levitt (Seattle: Broken Moon Press, 1992).

When preparing vegetables or soup . . . (p. 56)

From Dogen's "Instruction for the Tenzo." Translated by Arnold Kotler and Kazuaki Tanahashi. Reprinted with permission from *Moon in a Dewdrop,* edited by Kazuaki Tanahashi (San Francisco: North Point Press, 1985).

Zhaozhou asked a newly arrived monk . . . (p. 56)

This story was quoted in Dogen's "Everyday Activity," in *Treasury of the True Dharma Eye*. Translated by Katherine Thanas and Kazuaki Tanahashi. Reprinted with permission from *Moon in a Dewdrop*, edited by Kazuaki Tanahashi (San Francisco: North Point Press, 1985).

During my stay at Mt. Tiantong . . . (p. 57)

From Dogen's "Instruction for the Tenzo." Translated by Arnold Kotler and Kazuaki Tanahashi. Reprinted with permission from *Moon in a Dewdrop*, edited by Kazuaki Tanahashi (San Francisco: North Point Press, 1985).

Someone once asked Issan . . . (p. 58)

From *Street Zen: The Life Work of Issan Dorsey*, by Tensho David Schneider (Boston: Shambhala Publications, 1993).

To turn things while being turned by things . . . (p. 58)

From Dogen's "Instruction for the Tenzo." Translated by Arnold Kotler and Kazuaki Tanahashi. Reprinted with permission from *Moon in a Dewdrop*, edited by Kazuaki Tanahashi (San Francisco: North Point Press, 1985).

DAILY REMINDERS

Refuge Prayer (p. 60)

The Sangha is the third "gem" of Buddhism and the third source of refuge for Buddhists. Originally the Sangha meant the monks ordained by the Buddha himself—but now in general use the term encompasses the community of all Buddhists, ordained and lay practitioners both. Reprinted with permission from *Call Me by My True Names: The Collected Poems of Thich Nhat Hanh* (Berkeley: Parallax Press, 1993).

One and Many Engaged (p. 61)

This poem by Shitou Xiqian is recited in many Zen monasteries. Translated by Tom Cabarga, Philip Whalen, and Kazuaki Tanahashi.

Song of the Bright Mirror Samadhi (p. 63)

This poem by Dongshan Liangjie is chanted daily in many Zen monasteries. Translated by Tom Cabarga, Philip Whalen, and Kazuaki Tanahashi.

In Praise of Zazen (p. 67)

This poem is chanted daily in Rinzai monasteries in Japan. The Four Wisdoms are mirrorlike wisdom, wisdom of equanimity, discriminating-awareness wisdom, and all-accomplishing wisdom. Translated by the editors. Reprinted with permission from *Penetrating Laughter: Hakuin's Zen and Art*, by Kazuaki Tanahashi (Woodstock, NY: Overlook Press, 1984).

The Heart of the Prajnaparamita (p. 69)

Prajnaparamita is a Sanskrit term meaning "perfection of wisdom" or "undivided understanding." The term is also sometimes translated "wisdom gone beyond." The word *skandha* is Sanskrit for "heap." The five skandhas are the consituents of phenomena. These five are form, feeling, perception, mental formations, and consciousness. This text has been chanted for centuries in Zen and other Buddhist monasteries because of its emphasis on emptiness, and its cutting quality. Traditionally this teaching is presented as a dialogue between Avalokiteshvara Bodhisattva, the embodiment of enlightened compassion, and Shariputra, a sharp-minded disciple of Shakyamuni Buddha.

Mantras are generally not translated, as the sound itself is considered sacred, but the meaning can be interpreted as: "Gone, gone, gone beyond, completely gone beyond, Awakening, Hail!"

Translated by Thich Nhat Hanh. Reprinted with permission from *The Heart of Understanding: Commentaries on the Prajnaparamita Heart Sutra*, by Thich Nhat Hanh, edited by Peter Levitt (Berkeley: Parallax Press, 1988).

Gospel Noble Truths (p. 70)

Allen Ginsberg is a poet who lives in New York City. This poem is dated October 17, 1975. "Gospel Noble Truths" from *Collected Poems, 1947–1980* by Allen Ginsberg. Copyright © 1984 by Allen Ginsberg. Reprinted by permission of HarperCollins Publishers, Inc.

DEATH, GREAT DEATH

`The Suspense (p. 74)

Cid Corman is an American poet living in Kyoto. Reprinted with permission from *of*, by Cid Corman (Venice, CA: Lapis Press, 1990).

Having a body or not having a body . . . (p. 74)

Translated from Chinese by the editors.

Autumn valley . . . (p. 75)

Reprinted with permission from *Temple Dusk: Zen Haiku,* by Mitsu Suzuki, translated by Kazuaki Tanahashi and Gregory Wood (Berkeley: Parallax Press, 1992).

Dongshan had his head shaved . . . (p. 75)

From *Recorded Sayings of Dongshan.* Translated by the editors.

This sick pale face . . . (p. 76)

A Chinese-style poem by Daigu Ryokan. Translated by Daniel Leighton and Kazuaki Tanahashi.

For many years I dug the ground . . . (p. 76)

Muso Soseki (1275–1351) was a monk of the Rinzai School in Japan. This poem was written in 1305, upon his enlightenment. Translated by the editors.

Actualizing the Fundamental Point (p. 77)

The original title of this text is "Genjo Koan." Dogen gave this writing to his lay student in 1233 and revised it in 1252, one year before he died. It is one of the most revered Zen texts in the Soto School. Bokuzan Nishiari, a renowned Soto monk and scholar, referred to it in his lecture given in 1922: "This fascicle is the skin, flesh, bone, and marrow of the Founder. The fundamental dharma throughout his lifetime is revealed in this work. The ninety-five fascicles of the *Treasury of the True Dharma Eye* are the offshoots of this fascicle." Translated by Robert Aitken and Kazuaki Tanahashi, and revised at San Francisco Zen Center. From *Moon in a Dewdrop,* edited by Kazuaki Tanahashi (San Francisco: North Point Press, 1985).

Narrow path toward the cemetery . . . (p. 81)

Reprinted with permission from *Temple Dusk: Zen Haiku,* by Mitsu Suzuki, translated by Kazuaki Tanahashi and Gregory Wood (Berkeley: Parallax Press, 1992).

Birth, old age . . . (p. 82)

Ly Ngoc Kieu (1041–1113) is the earliest known female writer in Vietnam. She was a nun and monastery director. Translated by Thich Nhat Hanh and Jane Hirshfield. Excerpt from *Women in Praise of the Sacred: Forty-three Centuries of Spiritual Poetry by Women,* edited by Jane Hirshfield. Copyright © 1994 by Jane Hirshfield. Reprinted by permission of HarperCollins Publishers, Inc.

Death Poem (p. 83)

Translated by the editors.

My passport should be returned . . . (p. 83)

Translated from Japanese by Eido Shimano Roshi. Reprinted with permission from *Like a Dream, Like a Fantasy: The Zen Writings and Translations of Nyogen Senzaki,* edited by Eido Shimano (Tokyo: Japan Publications, 1978).

Full Moon in the Eighth Month (Death Poem) (p. 84)

A *waka* by Eihei Dogan. Translated by Brian Unger and Kazuaki Tanahashi. Reprinted with permission from *Moon in a Dewdrop,* edited by Kazuaki Tanahashi (San Francisco: North Point Press, 1985).

GRANDMOTHER'S HEART

Beneficial action is skillfully to benefit . . . (p. 86)

From "Bodhisattva's Four Methods of Guidance," in *Treasury of the True Dharma Eye.* Translated by Lew Richmond and Kazuaki Tanahashi. Reprinted with permission from *Moon in a Dewdrop,* edited by Kazuaki Tanahashi (San Francisco: North Point Press, 1985).

Please Call Me by My True Names (p. 86)

Reprinted with permission from *Call Me by My True Names: The Collected Poems of Thich Nhat Hanh* (Berkeley: Parallax Press, 1993).

Season's first tea fire . . . (p. 88)

Reprinted with permission from *Temple Dusk: Zen Haiku,* by Mitsu Suzuki, translated by Kazuaki Tanahashi and Gregory Wood (Berkeley: Parallax Press, 1992).

One life—too lazy to do anything! . . . (p. 89)

Translated from Chinese by the editors.

Layman Pang was sitting in his grass-thatched hut . . . (p. 89)

This Chinese story refers to Pangyan, a student of Mazu Daoyi. Translated by the editors.

When Dongshan was holding a memorial feast . . . (p. 90)

Yunyan Tansheng (782–841) studied with one teacher (Baizhang Huaihai) for twenty years, and then another (Yaoshan Weiyan), from whom he inherited dharma. Dongshan had many great teachers, several of them more famous than Yunyan, but here he describes his reasons for venerating this particular master. From *Recorded Sayings of Dongshan.* Translated by the editors.

The Fifth Ancestor of Zen in China . . . (p. 90)

This story about the Fifth (Daman Hongren) and Sixth (Dajian Huineng) Ancestors of Zen in China is found in *The Sixth Ancestor's Platform Sutra.* Translated by the editors. See also the note for "The Sixth Ancestor Huineng . . ." on p. 164.

Once Yunmen said to the assembly . . . (p. 92)

Yunmen Wenyan (864–949) became a dharma heir of Xuefeng Yicun and, after traveling widely, established a monastery that grew to one thousand monks. He is regarded as the founder of the Yunmen School, one of the famous Five Schools of Zen in China. From *Blue Cliff Record,* case 87. Translated by the editors.

Hymnus ad Patrem Sinensis (p. 92)

Zenshin Philip Whalen is a poet and the abbot of Issanji, One Mountain Temple, in San Francisco. This poem is dated September 21, 1963. Reprinted with permission from *On Bear's Head,* by Philip Whalen (New York: Harcourt, Brace & World, 1969).

Explaining a koan to Satsu . . . (p. 93)

Reprinted with permission from *Penetrating Laughter: Hakuin's Zen and Art,* by Kazuaki Tanahashi (Woodstock, NY: Overlook Press, 1984).

Students of the Way . . . (p. 94)

Quoted from *Treasury of the True Dharma Eye: Record of Things Heard,* compiled by Koun Ejo. Translated by the editors.

The beauty of these children is such . . . (p. 94)

Norman Fischer is a poet and abbot of San Francisco Zen Center. This poem was written in February 1978 at Tassajara Zen Mountain Center. Reprinted with permission from *Wind Bell,* summer 1983.

One day Maurine . . . (p. 95)

Maurine Stuart (1922–1990) taught at Cambridge Buddhist Meditation Center in Massachusetts. Her teachings will be presented in a forthcoming book entitled *Subtle Sound: The Zen Teachings of Maurine Stuart,* edited by Sherry Chayat. This story, by Basya Petnick, is reprinted with permission from *Turning Wheel,* spring 1990.

GREAT DOUBT

Xingyan said, "Suppose you were high up . . ." (p. 98)

Xingyan Zhixian (d. 898) was a Chinese teacher who was sweeping the graveyard of an old master when he was enlightened by the sound of a pebble striking bamboo. From *Gateless Barrier*, case 5. Translated by the editors.

Ekaku (Hakuin) gave up sleeping . . . (p. 98)

Dokyo Etan (1642–1721), Hakuin's main teacher, lived secluded in a mountain hut. Although he was not actively teaching at the time of this story, Hakuin had sought him out. Reprinted with permission from *Penetrating Laughter: Hakuin's Zen and Art*, by Kazuaki Tanahashi (Woodstock, NY: Overlook Press, 1984).

Wuzu said, "A water buffalo . . ." (p. 99)

Wuzu Fayan (d. 1104) was a Chinese monk of the Linji School. From *Gateless Barrier*, case 38. Translated by the editors.

Most of the work with a koan takes place alone . . . (p. 99)

Reprinted with permission from *Mountain Record of Zen Talks*, by John Daido Loori (Boston: Shambhala Publications, 1988).

The Sixth Ancestor Huineng came across . . . (p. 100)

Dajian Huineng (638–713), the Sixth Ancestor of Zen in China, was born to a poor family, and sold firewood for a living. One day in the market he heard monks chanting lines from the Diamond Sutra and became enlightened. Some time later, he joined the community of Daman Hongren (688–761), the Fifth Ancestor, where he served for eight months threshing rice. The Fifth Ancestor recognized his potential, however, and in a secret ceremony gave him dharma transmission. Hongren then urged him to flee, knowing that transmission to a poor, illiterate novice would cause dissension and anger in his community.

Huineng hid for years, sometimes even living with hunters, but finally became a teacher of great skill, with many important students. His teaching, known as the Southern School of Zen, emphasized immediate enlightenment, as distinct from the Northern School, which taught a path of gradual attainment.

From *Gateless Barrier*, compiled in China by Wumen Huikai in 1249; case 29. Translated by the editors.

In traditional Zen centers which work with sitting . . . (p. 101)

Reprinted with permission from *The Work of This Moment,* by Toni Packer (Springwater, NY: Springwater Center, 1988).

Once a monk called Director Xuanze . . . (p. 101)

Fayan Wenyi (885–955) was a founder of the Fayan School, one of the Five Schools of Chinese Zen. Baoen Xuanze was his student and dharma heir. From Dogen's "On the Endeavor of the Way," in *Treasury of the True Dharma Eye.* Translated by Ed Brown and Kazuaki Tanahashi. Reprinted with permission from *Moon in a Dewdrop,* edited by Kazuaki Tanahashi (San Francisco: North Point Press, 1985).

Soft spring rain . . . (p. 102)

Translated by Eido Shimano Roshi. From *The Soen Roku: The Sayings and Doings of Master Soen* (New York: Zen Studies Society Press, 1986).

Under the trees, among the rocks . . . (p. 102)

Translated by the editors.

Scalding coffee . . . (p. 103)

An English haiku, titled "Rohatsu Sesshin at Tassajara" by Lou Hartman.

Emperor Wu of Liang invited layman Fu . . . (p. 103)

Emperor Wu (464–549) was the first emperor of Liang, the Southern Kingdom of China. Lay teacher Fu (497–569), who studied with Bodhidharma, had a correspondence with the emperor, and was invited to come teach at the palace. From *Blue Cliff Record,* case 67. Translated by the editors.

Word will be destroyed by word . . . (p. 103)

From *The Dirty Mop: Unlimited Action Paintings and Poems by Jung Kwung, the Mad Monk,* text by Lewis R. Lancaster, poems translated by Paik Seung-Gil (Berkeley, CA: Asian Humanities Press, 1983).

No Matter, Never Mind (p. 104)

Gary Snyder, *Turtle Island.* © 1974 by Gary Snyder. Reprinted by permission of New Directions Publishing Corporation.

Self-portrait (p. 104)

Translated by the editors.

When you paint spring . . . (p. 106)

From Dogen's "Plum Blossoms," in *Treasury of the True Dharma Eye.* Translated by Sojun Mel Weitsman and Kazuaki Tanahashi. Reprinted with permission from *Moon in a Dewdrop*, edited by Kazuaki Tanahashi (San Francisco: North Point Press, 1985).

On His Self-Portrait (p. 106)

Reprinted with permission from *Penetrating Laughter: Hakuin's Zen and Art,* by Kazuaki Tanahashi (Woodstock, NY: Overlook Press, 1984).

One day a student asked Taiga Ike . . . (p. 107)

Taiga Ike (1723–1776) was one of the most accomplished painters of the Bunjin (literal-style) School in Japan. This school used Chinese-style subject matter and poetry, but carried out the work with Japanese sensitivity. Translated by the editors.

Where beauty is, then there is ugliness . . . (p. 107)

A Chinese-style poem by Daigu Ryokan. Translated by Daniel Leighton and Kazuaki Tanahashi.

Not last night . . . (p. 108)

Translated by the editors.

D. T. Suzuki, when I was studying with him . . . (p. 108)

Daisetz Teitaro Suzuki (1870–1966) was born in Japan and first came to the United States in 1897. A student of Rinzai Zen, he founded the Zen Studies Society in New York, and was a professor at Columbia University. His prolific writings, both in Japanese and in English, were in large measure responsible for the contemporary worldwide understanding of Zen.

John Cage (1912–1992) studied with D. T. Suzuki at Columbia, and later became one of the foremost avant-garde composers of the twentieth century. From "John Cage: The Music of Contingency, An Interview," *Zero*, vol. III. Copyright © 1979 by Zero Press.

Within This Tree (p. 109)

Jane Hirshfield is a longtime student of Soto Zen. Her most recent book of poetry is *The October Palace* (New York: HarperCollins, 1994), and her most recent anthology is *Women in Praise of the Sacred: Forty-three Centuries of Spiritual*

Poetry by Women (New York: HarperCollins, 1994). Excerpt from *The October Palace* by Jane Hirshfield. Copyright © 1994 by Jane Hirshfield. Reprinted by permission of HarperCollins Publishers, Inc.

A room for the way of tea ... (p. 109)

Jo'o Takeno (1504–1555) was an early forerunner of *wabi*-style (austere) tea ceremony in Japan. This style was influenced by Zen monastic life and developed separately from the elaborate, aristocratic style used to serve the nobility. Translated by the editors.

A tea spoon should be made in the way ... (p. 110)

Rikyu Sen (1520–91) established and formalized the *wabi*-style tea ceremony rituals in Japan. Translated by the editors.

Those who are nothing particular ... (p. 110)

Linji Yixuan (d. 867) was the founder of the Linji School in China. A brilliant and provocative teacher whose style included yelling and hitting, Linji produced twenty-two dharma heirs. From the *Recorded Sayings of Linji*, translated by the editors.

The way of tea has nothing to do with discriminating ... (p. 110)

Sotan Sen (1578–1658) was a Zen practitioner and tea master in the *wabi*-style school in Japan. He transmitted tea teaching to his three sons, each of whom developed a particular style. These three styles in turn became the major schools of tea ceremony. Translated by the editors.

When mountains and waters are painted ... (p. 110)

From Dogen's "Painting of a Rice-Cake," in *Treasury of the True Dharma Eye*. Translated by Dan Welch and Kazuaki Tanahashi. Reprinted with permission from *Moon in a Dewdrop*, edited by Kazuaki Tanahashi (San Francisco: North Point Press, 1985).

Who calls my poems poems? (p. 111)

A Chinese-style poem by Daigu Ryokan. Translated by Daniel Leighton and Kazuaki Tanahashi.

A good player of shakuhachi is ... (p. 111)

Fuyo Hisamatsu was an eighteenth-century shakuhachi player in Japan. The shakuhachi is a bamboo flute, played vertically. The Fuke school of Zen used begging and shakuhachi playing as their main practices. Reprinted with permission from "The Hitori Mondo (Self Dialogue) of Hisamatsu Fuyo," translated by Robin Hartshorne and Kazuaki Tanahashi, *Annals of the International Shakuhachi Society,* vol. 1.

To have nothing in mind is noble . . . (p. 112)
Translated by the editors.

Kobun Chino Roshi, a Zen master . . . (p. 112)
Adapted from a talk by Shunpo Blanche Hartman, San Francisco Zen Center. *Wind Bell,* fall 1993.

Issan Dorsey was asked, "What is the essence . . ." (p. 113)
Issan Dorsey (1933–1990) founded and taught at Hartford Street Zen Center, Issanji, in San Francisco. This story was collected in 1983.

An audience sometimes comments . . . (p. 113)
Zeami is an artist name for Motokiyo Kanze (1353–1443), a Noh actor and writer as well as a student of Zen. This quotation is from "Flower Mirror." Translated from Japanese by the editors.

THE KNOT

Yesterday by the river I saw trees . . . (p. 116)
Translated from Chinese by the editors.

The existence of disability . . . (p. 116)
An *oryoki* is a wrapped set of nested eating bowls. Meals taken in these bowls are eaten in a spiritual way. Joan Tollifson, who describes herself as a "one-armed seeker of truth," has enjoyed many oryoki meals. She lives and works at Springwater Center in New York. Reprinted with permission from "Imperfection Is a Beautiful Thing," by Joan Tollifson, *Buddhist Peace Fellowship,* fall 1990.

In the early 1980s when a movement . . . (p. 117)
Reprinted with permission from "The Original Line: Another Zen Paradox," by Kazuaki Tanahashi, *Alphabet,* vol. 11, no. 3 (1988).

When people talk about war . . . (p. 117)
Reprinted with permission from *The Dragon Who Never Sleeps: Verses for Zen Buddhist Practice,* by Robert Aitken (Berkeley: Parallax Press, 1992).

Spel Against Demons (p. 118)
Gary Snyder, *Turtle Island*, © 1974 by Gary Snyder. Reprinted by permission of New Directions Publishing Corporation.

Once an envoy from Emperor Dezong came . . . (p. 120)
Mingzan (eighth century) escaped the Chinese government's persecution of Buddhists and lived in seclusion on Mount Heng. He was known as Lazy Zan. The emperor and his emissary in this story are from a different government than the one that carried out the persecutions. From *Blue Cliff Record*, case 34. Translated by the editors.

Don't scold or criticize monks . . . (p. 120)
From *Treasury of the True Dharma Eye: Record of Things Heard*, compiled by Koun Ejo. Translated by the editors.

A purple robe—perfect for the "Zen Master" . . . (p. 121)
The title of this poem is "Celebrating the Occasion of the Monk Yoso of the Daiyu (Great Function) Temple Receiving the Imperial Title Zen Master Soe Daisho." This imperial title and the purple robe could be given only by the emperor. Ikkyu's poem is an attack; he uses sarcasm and wordplay to criticize his dharma brother for accepting such worldly honors. Translated by the editors.

The aspect of Zen in which I am personally interested . . . (p. 121)
Alan Watts (1915–1973) grew up in England and came to New York in the 1930s. He began to study Zen with Sokei-an Sasaki, and also became an Anglican priest. His extensive writings, lectures, and radio talks helped to popularize Zen and Taoism in the West. Reprinted with permission from the introduction to *Beat Zen, Square Zen*, by Alan Watts (San Francisco: City Lights Books, 1959).

Thich Nhat Hanh said at Plum Village . . . (p. 122)
Reprinted with permission from *33 Fingers: A Collection of Modern American Koans*, by Michael Wenger (San Francisco: Clear Glass Press, 1994).

One of the things that is realized . . . (p. 122)
Reprinted with permission from *Mountain Record of Zen Talks*, by John Daido Loori (Boston: Shambhala Publications, 1988).

How pleasant was the body of Chaos . . . (p. 122)
Translated from Chinese by the editors.

For Warmth (p. 123)
Reprinted with permission from *Call Me by My True Names: The Collected Poems of Thich Nhat Hanh* (Berkeley: Parallax Press, 1993).

In 1951 at Yale University, Sensei had gone . . . (p. 124)
Sensei is a Japanese term meaning "teacher." Reprinted with permission from "Reminiscences of Dr. Suzuki," in *A Zen Life: D. T. Suzuki Remembered,* photographs by Francis Haar, edited by Masao Abe (New York and Tokyo: Weatherhill, 1986).

A certain Zen teacher celebrated with his students . . . (p. 124)
Adapted from *Nine-Headed Dragon River Zen Journals 1969–85,* Peter Matthiessen (Boston: Shambhala Publications, 1985).

The more we sit like this . . . (p. 125)
Dainin Katagiri Roshi (1928–1990) was a Soto monk from Japan. He came to San Francisco in 1965 to assist Shunryu Suzuki Roshi, and he taught with him for several years at San Francisco Zen Center. After Suzuki Roshi's death, Katagiri Roshi founded the Minnesota Zen Meditation Center in Minneapolis. Reprinted with permission from *Returning to Silence,* by Dainin Katagiri (Boston: Shambhala Publications, 1988).

There doesn't have to be a need to solve anything . . . (p. 125)
From "A Vow of Service: Zen Practice and Social Responsibility," by Bernard Tetsugen Glassman. Reprinted with permission from *Mountain Record,* spring 1992.

With tropical forests in danger . . . (p. 125)
Reprinted with permission from *The Dragon Who Never Sleeps: Verses for Zen Buddhist Practice,* by Robert Aitken (Berkeley: Parallax Press, 1992).

While Sick (p. 126)
Translated by the editors.

My Teacher once said to me . . . (p. 126)
Gary Snyder, *Turtle Island,* © 1974 by Gary Snyder. Reprinted by permission of New Directions Publishing Corporation.

MOUNTAINS AND WATERS

There are mountains hidden in treasures . . . (p. 128)
From Dogen's "Mountains and Waters Sutra," in *Treasury of the True Dharma Eye*. Translated by Arnold Kotler and Kazuaki Tanahashi. Reprinted with permission from *Moon in a Dewdrop*, edited by Kazuaki Tanahashi (San Francisco: North Point Press, 1985).

Pine Tree Tops (p. 128)
Gary Snyder, *Turtle Island*, © 1974 by Gary Snyder. Reprinted by permission of New Directions Publishing Corporation.

Zen Telegram (p. 129)
Paul Reps (1895–1990) was a painter, poet, writer, and translator who worked with Nyogen Senzaki. Reps's book *Zen Flesh Zen Bones* introduced a number of koans and enigmatic Zen stories to a wide audience. Reprinted with permission from *Zen Telegram*, by Paul Reps (Tokyo: Charles E. Tuttle, 1959).

One day a young monk at Ryutaku-ji . . . (p. 129)
A *kensho* is a Japanese term meaning an awakening, an opening, a realization; applied to a breakthrough in koan study, it is sometimes called an "enlightenment experience." Reprinted with permission from *Nine-Headed Dragon River: Zen Journals, 1969–1985*, by Peter Matthiessen (Boston: Shambhala Publications, 1985).

Message to a monk who scribbles verse (p. 130)
Translated by the editors.

Spring has hundreds . . . (p. 130)
Wumen Huikai (1183–1260) was a Linji School monk in China. He compiled *Gateless Barrier*. From *Gateless Barrier*, case 19. Translated by the editors.

Man is but a part of the fabric of life . . . (p. 130)
Gary Snyder, *Turtle Island*, © 1974 by Gary Snyder. Reprinted by permission of New Directions Publishing Corporation.

On the broad river . . . (p. 131)
A Chinese-style poem by Daigu Ryokan. Translated by Daniel Leighton and Kazuaki Tanahashi.

It is not only that there is water . . . (p. 131)

From Dogen's "Mountains and Waters Sutra," in *Treasury of the True Dharma Eye.* Translated by Arnold Kotler and Kazuaki Tanahashi. Reprinted with permission from *Moon in a Dewdrop,* edited by Kazuaki Tanahashi (San Francisco: North Point Press, 1985).

Daowu visited the assembly of Shitou . . . (p. 132)

Tianghuang Daowu (748–807). This story was quoted by Dogen in "Going Beyond Buddha," in *Treasury of the True Dharma Eye.* Translated by Sojun Mel Weitsman and Kazuaki Tanahashi. Reprinted with permission from *Moon in a Dewdrop,* edited by Kazuaki Tanahashi (San Francisco: North Point Press, 1985).

Without desire everything is sufficient . . . (p. 132)

A Chinese-style poem by Daigu Ryokan. Translated by Daniel Leighton and Kazuaki Tanahashi.

Roshi (p. 133)

Leonard Cohen is a Zen student, poet, and songwriter who lives in Los Angeles. The roshi here is Joshu Sasaki Roshi, a Rinzai School monk from Japan who travels widely, teaching and leading sesshins. He has centers in Los Angeles and Mt. Baldy, California. From "Death of a Lady's Man" by Leonard Cohen, © 1968. Used by permission. All rights reserved.

Sound of mountain . . . (p. 134)

Translated by Sherry Chayat and Kazuaki Tanahashi.

CIRCLE

Shunryu Suzuki was gravely sick . . . (p. 136)

This story was told in direct conversation by Richard Baker Roshi, who was the student in question here.

The great road has no gate . . . (p. 136)

By Tiantong Rujing; quoted by Dogen in "All-Inclusive Study," in *Treasury of the True Dharma Eye.* Gautama is the historical Buddha Shakyamuni's family name. Translated by Sojun Mel Weitsman and Kazuaki Tanahashi. Reprinted with permission from *Moon in a Dewdrop,* edited by Kazuaki Tanahashi (San Francisco: North Point Press, 1985).

Go sit on the sixteenth-night koan . . . (p. 136)

A Chinese-style poem by Eihei Dogen. Translated by Philip Whalen and Kazuaki Tanahashi. Reprinted with permission from *Moon in a Dewdrop*, edited by Kazuaki Tanahashi (San Francisco: North Point Press, 1985).

The refreshing air wells up . . . (p. 137)

Shunpo Blanche Hartman teaches at San Francisco Zen Center. This poem is from statements made at the conclusion of a sesshin. Reprinted with permission from *Wind Bell*, winter 1983.

We go into the darkness . . . (p. 137)

Joan Halifax is a Zen teacher and anthropologist who teaches at the Upaya Foundation in Santa Fe. Excerpts from *The Fruitful Darkness*, by Joan Halifax. Copyright © 1993 by Joan Halifax. Reprinted by permission of HarperCollins Publishers, Inc.

Ed Brown: What power will you use . . . (p. 138)

This dialogue took place as part of the installation ceremony of Sojun Mel Weitsman as abbot of the Berkeley Zen Center. From *Wind Bell*, fall 1985.

Nanquan, Guizong, and Mayu were on their way . . . (p. 138)

Nanquan Puyan (748–834), Guizong Zhichang (eighth century), and Mayu Baoche (eighth century) were all students of Mazu Daoyi (709–788), who was considered one of the two "great jewels" of Zen in China (the other was Shitou). He had 130 enlightened disciples. He also started the tradition of "recorded sayings"—that is, the documenting of the sayings and teachings of a master who had just died. From *Blue Cliff Record*, case 69. Translated by the editors.

A monk asked Quianfeng, "It is said . . ." (p. 138)

Quianfeng was a ninth-century monk of the Caodong School in China. Little is known about him, other than that he was a dharma heir of Dongshan Liangjie. From *Gateless Barrier*, case 48. Translated by the editors.

Circular Portrait: Ikkyu and Mori (p. 139)

Mori, as the poem states, was a blind singer, with whom Ikkyu had a love affair late in his life. Xutang Zhiyu (1185–1269), a monk of the Linji School in China, was Ikkyu's dharma ancestor. Though this monk preceded him by a few generations, Ikkyu felt a close affinity with him, even going so far as to suggest that he, Ikkyu, was a reincarnation of Xutang. Translated by the editors.

On Opening the Ring of Bone Zendo (p. 139)

The Ring of Bone Zendo was originally built by Gary Snyder on San Juan Ridge, in California. The name was taken from a poem, "Ring of Bone," by the late Lew Welch. The name also serves as the title of Welch's collected poems. This poem by Robert Aitken Roshi is reprinted with permission from *Blind Donkey*, July 1986.

Ten Ox Herding Pictures (p. 141)

Kuoan Shiyuan was a twelfth-century monk of the Yangqi School in China. The ten ox-herding pictures compose a traditional metaphor for the stages of Zen practice, which have been portrayed over the centuries in paintings and poetry. Although several earlier portrayals of these stages had been made, Kuoan's became the most famous among Japanese monks. Translated by John Daido Loori and Kazuaki Tanahashi.

On the great road of buddha ancestors . . . (p. 144)

From Dogen's "Continuous Practice," in *Treasury of the True Dharma Eye*. Translated by the editors.